Coaching Football's Invert Defense

Coaching Football's
Invert Defense

Ralph Kirchenheiter

Parker Publishing Company, Inc.
West Nyack, N.Y.

Library of Congress Cataloging in Publication Data

Kirchenheiter, Ralph
    Coaching football's invert defense.

    1. Football--Defense. 2. Football coaching.
I. Title.
GV951.1.K55   796.33'22   73-12080
ISBN 0-13-139295-6

Dedicated to my wife, Andrea, and our children, Susan and Chris. They have graciously allowed football to bring our family closer together.

What's in This Book for You

Winning consistently is a basic goal of all coaches at all levels. At the high school level, however, there are several unique problems confronting the coach, including those of motivation, personnel, staff utilization and program development. Yet certain coaches and certain teams, in spite of these problems, seem to be winners year in and year out. We were fortunate enough to be part of such a program, and we learned much from the experience. The purpose of this book is to share with you the facts, principles and philosophies that accounted for our success. Equally as important, we emphasize how they are communicated to the squad.

Defense, in particular the Invert Defense, was the central theme from which our entire program radiated. It is a single defensive concept, flexible enough to be utilized from any place on the field and against all opponents, yet simple enough to be taught to every player by every coach on the staff.

As you would expect to find in any book on defense, we will outline in detail our methods of personnel selection, teaching techniques at every position, and our keys and coaching points for the entire scheme. This material is presented in a format that you'll find easily adaptable to your own playbook, if incorporating the entire Invert Defense into your own program is your desire. That, however, is only the bare skeleton of the text. Its real value is to the coach who is searching for the little extras that will provide his team with the winning edge.

Chapter 10, Invert Defense vs. the "Offense of the Seventies," is a highlight which deals in detail with our efforts to offset offensive trends in this decade. In addition, it includes a unique section on the most difficult runs and passes for Invert Defenses, which is absolutely "must" reading for any coach who will play or play against an Invert team next season. That includes all of us, as this scheme continues to grow in popularity.

For the first time in any book on defensive football, the concept of the Invert Triangle is clearly and concisely explained. This single most important principle of secondary play is what separates this pass defense from all others. It has been proven successful as employed by this coach in college as well as in high school.

From the goal line to 5-back coverages, from the kickoff to the extra point, not a single stone has been left unturned. We have included everything we ever did, from coaching our assistant coaches to game-by-game studies of every aspect of our defensive scheme.

Whether you buy the Invert Defense lock, stock and barrel, or are simply motivated to better understand our scheme and thus be better prepared to attack us offensively, we assure you that *Coaching Football's Invert Defense* will help make you a better coach.

Ralph Kirchenheiter

Acknowledgments

Because this book is about a particular football program it is necessary to point out from the beginning that it reflects the efforts of all those persons connected with the program. River Dell's origin lies in two cooperating communities, River Edge and Oradell, whose citizens have extended themselves to provide the best educational and extracurricular experiences for their children. Their support to the football program has traditionally been solid and broadbased. The fact that men like Tom Cahill and Mickey Corcoran were present to give an impetus to athletics at the school was important, but surely Matty Certosimo, Head Football Coach at River Dell when the Invert Defense started, is *the* most important personality in its football tradition. The coaches who served with me on Matty's staff, those who continued with me and the present staff—we are all indebted to him for the opportunity and direction he provided each of us. Men like Lars Larsen, Whitey Rightmire, Tom Godfrey, Dick Snyder, Lou Giglio, Rich Looram and many others have played an important role in developing the tradition of River Dell's Invert Defense. But undoubtedly the greatest praise and thanks must be reserved for the young men who represented their school throughout this period. They above all have made it what it is.

Coaches, like all professionals, are a product of their teachers. I have been fortunate in being exposed to several men whom I truly admire in the profession. Len Smith, my high school mentor, started the fires burning many years ago. Jim Brakefield, Defensive Coach at Wofford College while I was an undergraduate and presently Head Coach at Appalachian State University, taught me more about winning and the drive to win than anyone could ever hope to be taught. At River Dell, of course, it was Matty Certosimo who gave me the opportunity, confidence, and loyalty to grow with the Invert Defense. Finally I am indebted to Jim Root, Head Coach at the College of William and Mary, for allowing me to fulfill a lifelong ambition to coach football, the game I live and love, at the major college football level. The influence of each of these men is found throughout the text, and it is as much theirs as it is my own.

Finally, a third group of coaches must be acknowledged for their contributions—those who have shared their ideas with me through their writings and clinic presentations, or in informal conversations. While there is no way to acknowledge them all, gentlemen like Lee Royer, Bill Parcells, Drew Tallman and my William and Mary associate Lou Tepper have all had direct influences on this writing and their help is greatly appreciated.

Table of Contents

Coaching the Invert Defensive Secondary *(cont.)*

1

Defensive Flexibility
with the Invert Defense

The first thing that an offensive coach seeks in establishing his game plan is a physical mismatch, one that will allow his personnel to take advantage of a particular defender's limitations within the total defensive scheme. Recognition of potential strengths and weaknesses is probably the most important task of both offensive and defensive coaching. Nothing short of 12 men will provide an ideal defensive alignment, one in which all potentialities are accounted for; therefore, the defense must within its basic philosophy account for a need to hide its weaknesses. It was the inability to hide our personnel limitations that dictated our change, several years ago, to the Invert Defense.

THE NEED FOR INVERT DEFENSE WAS ESTABLISHED

River Dell High School, Oradell, New Jersey, had experienced a significant amount of success on the gridiron under the direction of Tom Cahill, who went on to become head coach at West Point, and Matty Certosimo, long recognized as one of New Jersey's finest mentors. It began to appear, however, that opposition offenses were catching up with the 5-2 Oklahoma defense that had been so successful. In particular, it became most difficult to annually find athletes capable of meeting the demands of the cornerback position. The cornerback was expected to confront aggressively an oncoming power sweep, with its onslaught of pulling guards and powerful fullbacks, and then, on the very next play, cover the best receiver on a deep pass pattern. Quite simply, this was the mismatch that offensive coaches were seeking, and very little could be done within the framework of the basic rotating secondary to compensate for it.

It was about this time that the Arkansas Monster defense was becoming popular, and along with it, various defensive alignments using "4 across the board" secondaries. Experimentation with looping and slanting lines, free-safety zones, man-to-man and invert zones became the major topic of conversation in college coaching circles. It was a matter of coincidence that Bill Parcells, currently Defensive Coach at Vanderbilt University and formerly one of River Dell's outstanding athletes, was playing on an Invert Defense at Wichita State University. When he returned home to visit, he expounded his praise of this particular alignment and established the foundations of River Dell's own version of the Invert.

THE INVERT CONCEPT

Traditionally, defenses using 7-man fronts would rotate their 4-man secondary up on movement of the ball to one side or the other. To accomplish this, the cornerback was required to play up to the flat (contain) on movement toward him, and deep-outside if the ball moved away (Figure 1-1).

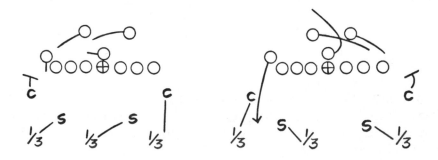

FIGURE 1-1

Rotating 4-Man Secondary

By exchanging the responsibilities of the safeties and corner-backs, and reversing the depth at which they initially align, the basic Invert Secondary is established (Figure 1-2).

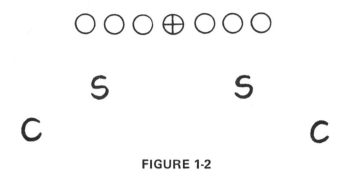

FIGURE 1-2

Basic Inverted Secondary

For simplicity, we renamed the respective positions, referring to the cornerbacks as halfbacks, since their responsibilities more closely relate to those of halfbacks in a 3-deep zone defense, and to the safeties as inverts, relating to cornerback responsibilities while aligned in the inside (inverted) position. While the halfback's position is more or less fixed in the deep outside zone, the inverts operate in tandem along a line called the Invert Triangle, alternately playing safety or cornerback according to the move-ment of a predetermined key (Figure 1-3). Detailed discussion of the Invert Triangle, probably the most important concept of invert secondary play, will be reserved for Chapter 6, Coaching the Invert

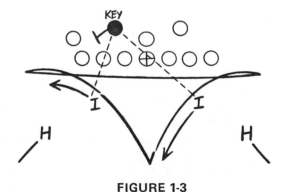

FIGURE 1-3

Movement Along the Invert Triangle

Defensive Secondary. For the present, it is sufficient to say that on movement of the ball, one invert will be coming up to defend the corner while the other retreats to defend the deep middle.

LOGICAL SUCCESSOR TO MONSTER DEFENSE

Far more than a mere variation in alignment of the defensive backs, the Invert Defense is flexible enough to contend with all offensive sets from all positions on the field. Improved scouting systems in the last decade had brought about the trend of using "unbalanced" defenses, such as the Arkansas Monster (Figure 1-4).

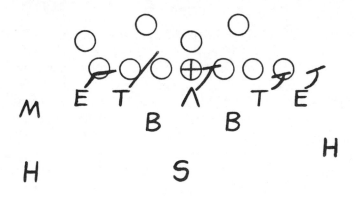

FIGURE 1-4

Arkansas Monster Defense

The Monster-type defenses established a strong side by placement of the "monster," then slanting the line away from him, essentially neutralizing the manpower advantage initially created. The Invert Defense, on the other hand, presents a balanced appearance, but on the snap of the ball the line is slanting to gain advantage to one side or the other. The inverts, reacting to a key, can react toward the slant, thus creating an overpowering manpower advantage, or opposite the slant of the line, again establishing a balanced front (Figure 1-5).

Invert Defenses owe much of their basic techniques and philosophy to the originators of the Monster Defense. However, we feel that the ability of the Invert Defense to hide its

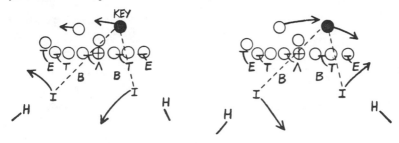

FIGURE 1-5

Inverts Can Support or Neutralize the Slant

declaration of strength, compensate for set variation and motion of backs, makes it the logical successor to the Monster in the never-ending trend of improving football.

INVERT DEFENSE MEASURES UP

Because our inability to adequately defend the corner and deep-pass route simultaneously initiated our study of the Invert Defense, it is reasonable to expect that we demanded much in this area from the defense. The initial deep-outside position of the halfbacks and their freedom from immediate run responsibility encouraged sound pass defense, so the Invert certainly measured up in that respect. The invert's ability to hide behind the defensive end and to take the wide sweep on an inside-out tackling angle made him a difficult target for pulling guards and fullbacks leading the play. We have found that it is practically impossible to run a sweep against our defense without a crackback block, regardless of how many blockers are leading the play. Consequently, we feel that the Invert Defense meets our standards for simultaneously defending the deep-pass and corner attack.

The second aspect of the Invert concept is what makes it so much fun to play. We are able to get a tremendous variety of stunts in the forcing unit while maintaining the simple pass defense. The variety of stunts that are practical and valuable to the forcing unit is almost limitless. Basically, we attempt to do two things with our stunts and games up front. First, we attempt to vary the look without varying the basic responsibilities, and second, we try to maintain the same initial look, yet change markedly the effective charges of the line. We feel that the Invert Defense, perhaps better than any other alignment, presents a varied front while maintaining a sound and simple pass defense.

Because it is predicated on movement, quickness, agility and team play, and not on size, the Invert Defense lends itself to the type of athlete most often found in high school football. We will discuss the particular physical requirements of each position as we discuss coaching those respective positions in later chapters, but quite simply, we feel you need four football players, the DEs and LBs; three wrestlers, the MG and inverts; two basketball players, HBs; and tackles who are more agile than big. We believe that we can find athletes annually to fulfill those qualifications; thus, on defense, we fit the players to the defense, whereas on offense, our philosophy has traditionally been to adapt the offense to the available talent. It is noteworthy, I suppose, that through the years our defense has been more consistent than our offense; perhaps this difference in philosophy accounts for this variation.

The fourth major facet of the Invert concept is the potential for having "unbalanced" defense without really showing it. This permits us to make better utilization of our scouting reports. When a particular offensive tendency is shown, we can make the call from within our normal defensive scope to capitalize on it. For example, one regular opponent over the years has shown a 95 percent tendency to roll-out right and pass on third and long. They'll use any variety of patterns, but point of attack is consistent. We have successfully defended this maneuver with the defensive call shown in Figure 1-6.

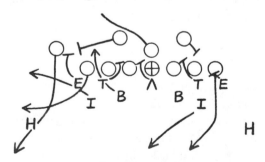

FIGURE 1-6

Chuckles Crossfire vs. Roll Right Pass

That leads us to the final, and probably most important, aspect of the Invert Defense. Within the scope of the defense lies the potential to align in 4, 5 and 6-man fronts and the flexibility to adjust to variations in sets, motion and offensive tendencies. The coach is equipped with a tool that offers the best of two major defensive philosophies. First, from a player's point of view, the defense is consistent. He knows it is tried and tested. He gets security from the fact that we have not had to abandon our defense in past years, and don't anticipate changing in the future. It was the No. One defense in the area during five of the eight seasons studied. The coach, on the other hand, has the flexibility to make weekly adjustments without, as they do in Multiple Defense, giving up the continuity that the players believe in. More than half of our game preparation time is spent on our defensive game plan. We feel that we possess within our defensive repertoire, variations that can be adapted to stop any offense.

THE INVERT DEFENSE VOCABULARY

The multiple number of alignments and the variations in our manner of attacking the offense revolve around a simple vocabulary list which is found in every player's notebook. We emphasize that each call is a coordinated effort of eleven men, each doing his job correctly. The elimination of mental errors is most important to us. Complete understanding of our defensive terminology is a requisite to having the privilege of playing on this highly successful unit. We test, on the field, regularly to see that every player understands his job on every call. Any tendency to make errors under those conditions essentially precludes a player's opportunity to play defense.

DEFENSIVE TERMINOLOGY

1. *Monster:* Basic defense, loop to *right* (Figure 1-7).
2. *Chuckles:* Basic defense, loop to *left* (Figure 1-8).
3. *Split-End Adjustments:* Adjustments in basic alignment to compensate for offensive SE. Normal, Eagle, and Cover are the three calls; they will be discussed later in detail.
4. *Hawk Defense:* Variation of basic alignment in which

the "hawk," a fifth defensive back, replaces a lineman. This call will be discussed in detail in Chapter 7. Scream'n Hawk is when the Hawk is used as a linebacker; Hawk is also our term for an interception.

5. *Goal-Line Monster* or *Chuckles, Rush* and *Goal-Line Pride:* Short-yardage and goal-line adjustments of regular defense. They are explained in Chapter 8.

6. *Mike:* Refers to Mikeman (middle guard), align in assigned gap and blow it, LB on that side stacks.

7. *Away:* Refers to the tackle away from the loop direction (away tackle), align in gap and blow it, LB to that side stacks.

8. *Gap:* Refers to Mike and away tackle, simultaneous Mike and away, both LBs stack.

9. *Fire:* LB (or LBs) straight fire of gap for which he is initially responsible. Fire-Right, Fire-Left, Double-Fire.

10. *Special Fire:* Mike loops opposite the call, away LB fires the center-guard gap to the side of loop (crosses behind Mike).

11. *Crossfire:* Loop tackle loops opposite the call, onside LB fires into offensive tackle-end gap.

12. *Blood:* Anchor end and away tackle blast down the line on 45° angle; their responsibility is to "make something happen."

13. *Eagle:* Tackle (or tackle and end) move in on initial alignment and linebacker sets to their outside, switching initial responsibilities.

The next five terms also affect the secondary:

14. *Pre-Invert:* Inverts' alignment along the triangle is moved up to one side (back from the other) so that one invert is initially aligned in the *up* position while the other is in the *deep* position.

15. *Revert:* Reversal of initial movement along the triangle due to reverse or bootleg action. Accomplished by calling "Revert" after play has started, or by declaring "Up" or "Deep" as key goes in motion.

16. *Thunder:* Invert away from loop fires the guard-tackle gap. The away tackle and anchor end loop opposite the

call. The other invert must cover deep-middle, no key. (This is our Safety-Blitz.)

17. *Hammer: Up* invert and HB to his side switch responsibilities. On movement of key, *up* invert goes to deep-outside and HB levels off to cover flat or contain sweep.

18. *3/4 Rotate:* From pre-inverted alignment, on flow away from *up* invert, the HB levels off, the *deep* invert rotates to the deep-outside and the *up* invert reverts back to the deep middle.

These last five terms will be explained in more detail in Chapter 6, while the others, those affecting the forcing unit, will be clarified at this time.

MONSTER—CHUCKLES, THE BASIC CALLS

Our forcing unit will be moving on every single play. Normally, over 50 percent of the calls will be the basic Monster, loop to the right call, or the Chuckles, loop to the left call. We are often asked, "Why don't you ever play it straight?" I can only answer that playing it straight would require teaching another technique to our linemen. Would the value derived from playing it straight merit the time spent to teach it? We feel it would not, and frankly, it might do some harm. For example, the technique for beating a double-team block differs for a slanting or looping lineman, compared to a lineman playing it straight.

The diagrams and comments in Figures 1-7 and 1-8 should give you a broad perspective of our basic calls.

VARY THE LOOK, NOT THE RESPONSIBILITY

Working from the regular 5-man front, we can vary our look by using the Mike, Away and Gap calls. In each case the respective lineman lines up in the gap to which he would normally have been looping, and the linebacker to his side stacks behind him. These three calls give us six slightly different looks (Figure 1-9), but don't change any basic responsibilities.

By using one of the above variations, we gain and lose certain advantages. A tackle, for example, aligned in the inside gap (an

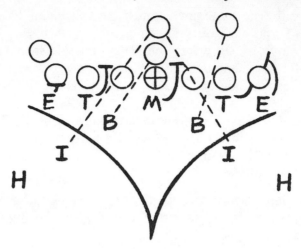

POSITION	TECHNIQUE	RESPONSIBILITY		
		play at you	play away from you	pass play
Right End	Loop Out	Quick Contain	Trail	Pressure Passer
Right Tackle	Outside Loop (SE adjust)	Control Off-Tackle area	Pursue	Cover Flat
Mike	Scoop Right	Make Something Happen	Pursue	Draw Screen Pressure
Left Tackle	Inside Loop (scoop)	Control Dive area	Pursue	Get the Passer—NOW
Left End	Anchor	Control Off-Tackle area	Search & Pursue	Pressure Outside Leverage
Right Linebacker	KEY: near setback Hit & Git	Scrape	Counter	Hook
Left Linebacker	KEY: QB Hit & Git	Scrape	Counter	Hook
Inverts	KEY: Back away from loop	*Up* reaction on triangle	*Deep* reaction on triangle	*Up*—flat *Deep*—deep middle
Halfbacks	Shuffle Key & Focus	Contain—come up outside cautiously	Deepest pursuit angle	Deep Outside get HAWK

FIGURE 1-7

Basic Responsibilities—Monster

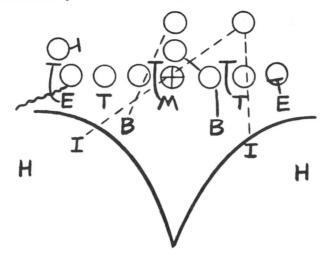

POSITION	TECHNIQUE	RESPONSIBILITY		
		play at you	play away from you	pass play
Right End	Anchor	Control Off-Tackle area	Search & Pursue	Pressure with Outside Leverage
Right Tackle	Inside Loop (scoop)	Control Dive area	Pursue	Get the Passer—NOW
Mike	Scoop Left	Make Something Happen	Pursue	Draw Screen Pressure
Left Tackle	Outside Loop (SE adjust)	Control Off-Tackle area	Pursue	Cover Flat
Left End	Loop Out	Quick Contain	Trail	Pressure Passer
Right Linebacker	KEY: QB Hit & Git	Scrape	Counter	Hook
Left Linebacker	KEY: Near setback Hit & Git	Scrape	Counter	Hook
Inverts	KEY: back away from loop	*Up* reaction on triangle	*Deep* reaction on triangle	*Up*—flat *Deep*—deep middle
Halfbacks	Shuffle Key & Focus	Contain—come up cautiously	Deepest pursuit angle	Deep Outside get HAWK

FIGURE 1-8

Basic Responsibilities—Chuckles

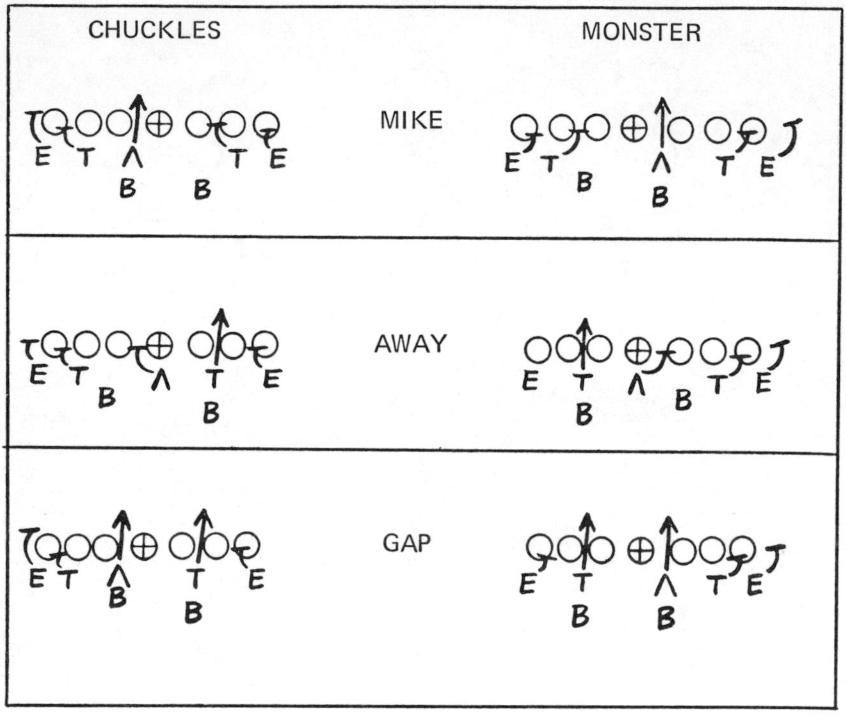

FIGURE 1-9

Varying the Look, Not the Responsibilities

Away call), is a more effective pass rusher, and can react to pressure from the outside on a run opposite the loop more easily than a tackle who is scooping down. If the opposing team has intended to "isolate" on the LB, or simply run a dive to that side, they will have a more difficult time. However, he has given up the surprise element. The line is now able to make blocking calls, knowing that the tackle will assume responsibility for the dive area, the Mikeman will be looping away from him, and the end to his side will be anchoring.

Our straight fires, Fire-Right, Fire-Left and Double-Fire, would also be included in this category. Essentially, the LB firing is filling the hole for which he had initial responsibility (Figure 1-10). The advantage of straight firing is usually limited to two basic offensive maneuvers. We have found it very effective to fire against teams that pull their guards often, and teams that run a lot of "isolation" type plays.

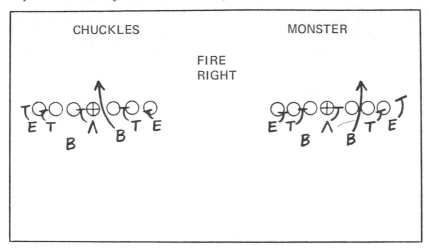

FIGURE 1-10a

Mon/Chuc Fire Right

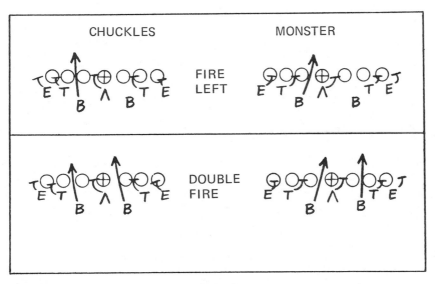

FIGURE 1-10 b, c

Mon/Chuc Fire Left and Double Fire

VARY THE RESPONSIBILITY, NOT THE LOOK

Used more effectively in creating long-yardage situations are stunts in the forcing unit in which the basic alignment is normal, but the charge of the line and coverages of our linebackers are varied. Cross charges, involving linebackers, are accomplished with the Crossfire (Figure 1-11) and the Special Fire (Figure 1-12) calls.

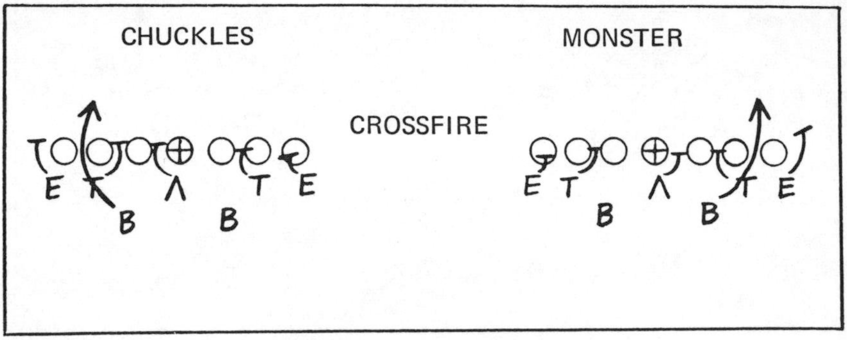

FIGURE 1-11

Mon/Chuc Crossfire

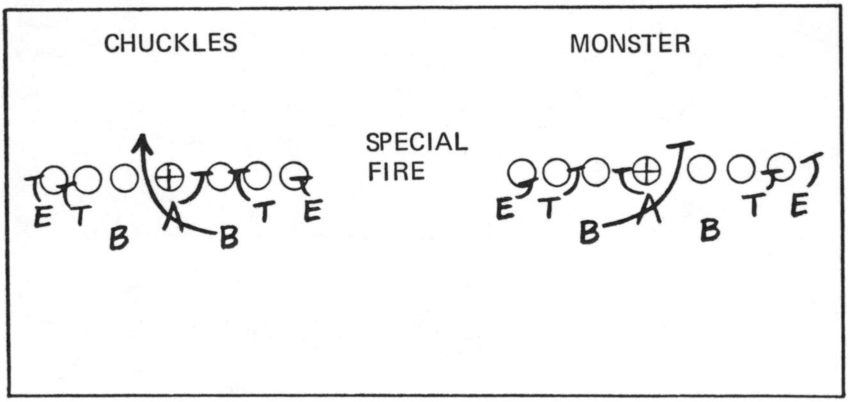

FIGURE 1-12

Mon/Chuc Special Fire

It should be noted that the linebacker not involved in the call would be free to fire also, and I'm sure that idea would appeal to many of you. Our philosophy on the matter, however, is that our linebackers represent the best football players on our team. They have been selected because of their ability to seek out and destroy enemy ballcarriers, and we hate to commit both of them on a prescribed path at the same time. We prefer instead to create pressure at one particular point in the offensive line, and use the other linebacker in a safer manner. The Crossfire has proven particularly successful against sprint-out and roll-out type teams, while the Special Fire is our best drop-back pass rushing alignment.

The second type of stunt used to vary the responsibility without changing the look is used predominantly on the hashmarks. It is simply a Blood call on which we slant the away tackle and anchor end down to their inside with reckless abandon. The sideline offers sufficient support to our backside defenders, and the pressure inside and pursuit of these linemen make this a very effective hashmark call (Figure 1-13a and b).

FIGURE 1-13a

Monster Blood

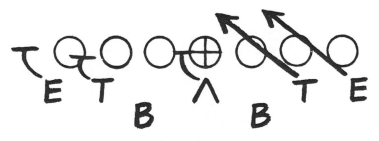

FIGURE 1-13b

Chuckles Blood

We don't often combine calls, as we fear it might prove confusing. However, there are times when particular combinations of stunts have proven particularly effective. On a short-yardage down, with the ball on the defensive right hashmark, Chuckles-

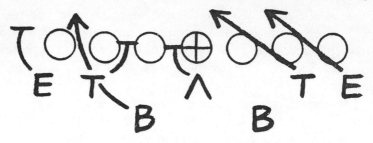

FIGURE 1-14

Chuckles-Blood-Crossfire

Blood-Crossfire has been successful more often than once (Figure 1-14).

Other stunts in the forcing unit require a variation in the alignment to a 4 or 6-man front or the inclusion of the secondary in the stunting activity. For the sake of clarity, the explanations of these variations will be reserved for the respective chapters to which they apply.

SPLIT-END ADJUSTMENTS

Because of the regularity with which we now see split-ends, we found it desirable to establish a set of rules governing our adjustments to them. A split-end is defined as an offensive end separated five or more yards from the offensive tackle, *without* a back set outside that tackle. These adjustments therefore do not apply to slot formations or any twin wide receivers. The purpose, as expressed to the athletes, is to take advantage of an offensive weakness. When the offense splits an end, it reduces its blocking strength off-tackle to that side, spreads our secondary and reduces the effectiveness of our normal loop tackle or anchor end. We believe that we can gain an advantage over the offense when they split the end by making one of the three basic adjustments. Each adjustment has a purpose, and our linebackers, inverts, ends and tackles must understand why a particular adjustment is made.

The adjustment call is made by the linebacker to the side of the split-end. The call may immediately follow the defensive call in the huddle, if the formation can be anticipated, or on the line when the formation is shown. If the adjustment interferes with a stunt originally called, the stunt is merely checked off. Quite often, however, the stunt is not affected.

The three calls will be diagrammed against an end split to the defensive right, since this is the more common formation, but the mirror of these is equally applicable. Experience has shown us that the Eagle call will be used about 60 percent of the time, Normal about 30 percent and Cover the remaining 10 percent of the time.

NORMAL
Use: If *SE* is to the *wide side* of the field, and we anticipate a wide play or action pass to SE's side.
Alignment: Normal.
Technique: End—establish hard quick contain, lead with inside leg, attack QB on option.
Tackle—if loop to, Spy technique; loop away, normal scoop.
LB and Invert—normal reactions.

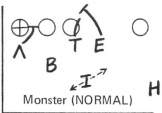

Monster (NORMAL)

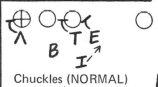

Chuckles (NORMAL)

EAGLE
Use: If *SE* is to *short side* of field, or if you anticipate an inside or strong side play or pass.
Alignment: Tackle and DE move in, line on guard and tackle respectively. LB aligns one yard behind the outside DE. Inverts pre-invert to formation.
Technique: Tackle and End—except for alignment play normal techniques.
LB—aligned 1 x 1 outside DE, key near setback, force through him on sprint action, cover him on drop-back; if he blocks, protect the curl zone.
Inverts—pre-invert to formation strength, key (FB) setback to formation.

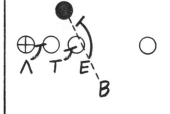

Monster (EAGLE)

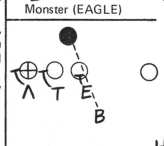

Chuckles (EAGLE)

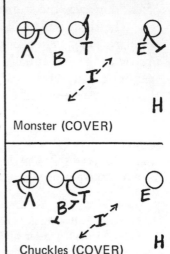

COVER
Use: Use in definite pass situations.
Alignment: DE align on inside shoulder of SE, all others align normally.
Technique: End—delay, force outside release, defend flat, look for screen or flare release to your side.
Tackle—loop away, scoop, loop to, contain.
LB—normal, but on play action to your side, scrape tough.
Inverts—normal alignment and keys.

Monster (COVER)

Chuckles (COVER)

DEFENSIVE PRIDE IS CONTAGIOUS

Having fun playing defensive football results from two different factors. First and foremost is success. We were fortunate to have particularly good athletes in our initial season with the Invert Defense and they set the tempo for defensive pride that has expanded each season. We attempt to capitalize on the past glories of defensive performers, and keep careful records of the accomplishments of each team and each player. An example of the kind of motivation that works in this way is the passing down of jersey numbers through successive classes. Every player to wear 65 in recent years has become a Team Captain in his senior year. Number 80 has brought us two All-County defensive ends in the last four years, and we have high hopes for a third in the near future. Pride has carried us through a few bare spots during the tenure of the Invert Defense, but it is pride well founded in quality performances.

Making a defense work is not only the result of good athletes; it also depends on communication of its basics from the coaching staff to the players. We have been fortunate in having a staff of coaches who were not only competent but also enthusiastic about what we were doing. Every coach believed in the quality of our program, and therefore could enthusiastically and honestly go out and sell it to our athletes.

2

Incorporating the Invert Defense
into the Practice Plan

Communication of football fundamentals from coach to player is the basis of any sound football program. A comparison of the storehouse of technical knowledge of highly successful and unsuccessful coaches, we propose, would not show any significant difference. But attending a single practice conducted by these same coaches would most likely produce accountable evidence for the difference in their records.

TWO-PLATOONING THE COACHING STAFF

A few years ago, the number of high school coaches working on their football program around the year was minimal. Today it is not only necessary for a coach to work a full calendar year, but to be successful, he must enlist the aid of his staff members during the off-season as well as in season.

River Dell football is indebted to Matty Certosimo for his many contributions to its fine tradition, but probably his greatest asset was his ability to spread the pleasures and rewards of winning to his staff. He was able to motivate his coaches and utilize their respective abilities, so that each coach felt that he was being recognized for his efforts and that River Dell Football reflected, in part, his own coaching.

37

We have worked with staffs of varying sizes during the past few years, and feel that we have now reached the optimum level of productivity for a school our size. Our seven-man coaching staff is organized in the following manner:

Ralph Kirchenheiter	Head Coach/linebackers
Dick Snyder	Offensive Coordinator/off. backs
Tom Godfrey	Defensive Coordinator/def. backs
Lou Giglio	JV-Soph Offense/linemen
Jim Lake	JV-Soph Defense/def. ends
Ken Burgess	Frosh Offense/linemen
John Stoehs	Frosh Defense/backs

The unique thing about these staff assignments, at the high school level, is the emphasis on offense/defense. We feel that offensive and defensive success is something that an assistant coach can identify with. When the defense registers a shutout, it is his defense, those are "his boys" that did the job. With opportunity for such identification, we can expect that the Defensive Coach is going to work just a little harder at his job.

Interestingly enough, two-platoon coaching at River Dell followed the introduction of the Invert Defense. Playing two-platoon football was something we always wanted to do, but it had seemed like a luxury we could not afford. The most surprising offshoot that developed from our change to the Invert Defense was that defensive specialization was encouraged. In the backfield particularly, athletes who appeared best qualified for the invert and halfback positions were usually not the best offensive backs. Consequently, as early as the freshman year, we began to filter off a defensive secondary that would exist as a unit through four years of the football program. Similarly, because the emphasis was on quickness and mobility in the defensive line, the bigger, less agile young players tended to be offensive linemen while the more aggressive linemen were slated for defensive play.

The only problem area, as far as platooning was concerned, was with linebackers and defensive ends. These boys, being our best athletes, often served as fullbacks or tight ends on offense, and their respective coaches fought for their presence in practice. By including tight ends with the defensive ends in group work, the problem of adequately distributing our coaching staff was limited to the fullback-linebacker problem. We accordingly allow the needs of our squad to determine in which group a boy will work.

DAILY PRACTICE SCHEDULE

A look at our daily practice schedule (Figure 2-1) confirms the offense-defense orientation of our coaching staff. The Offensive Coach works only with offensive players during the entire practice. In addition to his group work with offensive backs and split-ends, he assumes responsibility for the Raider (opposition) offense during our defensive teamwork. His direct handling of regular offensive players during this period assures the defense of a well-organized unit to defend, and not a disinterested group of misfits that often plague scout teams. The Defensive Coach, while directing the Raider defense against our offense, has the opportunity to give individual attention to regular defensive performers or to specialists on the second unit without taking away from his normal overall coaching assignment.

A closer look at our daily practice schedule gives some insight into our attitudes toward defensive football. We place a premium on individual quickness and movement, and our daily insistence on agility, reaction and key drills represents this emphasis. At the expense of overcrowding our dressing facilities, we installed a Universal Gym in our locker room and use it in season as well as out. Before they finish dressing, all varsity players, except quarterbacks, make a complete circuit on the machine, exercising with quick violent movements at 3/4 weight capacity for 15 seconds at each station. We feel that this training accomplishes two purposes. Combined with a once-a-week heavier lifting session, it serves to maintain strength throughout the season; and second, particularly in colder weather, it serves as a warm-up before the athletes go out to practice.

The first thing our players do when they get outside is a two-minute Flexibility Routine. We expect each of them to accomplish work during the opening Specialty Period of practice, and can not wait for Calisthenics for them to begin stretching out. The four exercises done on their own are:

1. *Leg Swing:* Lean against wall, swing leg through on an extended arc across your front and up to the side.

DAILY FOOTBALL PRACTICE SCHEDULE

S P E C I A L T Y	KIRCHENHEITER	LAKE	GIGLIO	GODFREY	SNYDER
	1. Personnel problems 2. Punt & KO Returns	1. QB & Receiver warm-up	1. Universal Gym & Flexibility 2. Linemen	1. Training Room 2. Kickers	1. Field Equipt. 2. Backs (blocking)
3	CALISTHENICS				
5	Agilities—LBs	Agilities—DEs	Agilities—Line	Agilities—Def Bks	Agilities—Off Backs
9	H/R | CAT / TRIANGLE / BUTT	H/R | TRIANGLE / BUTT / CAT	H/R | BUTT / CAT / TRIANGLE	DEFENSIVE SECONDARY FUNDAMENTALS	OFFENSIVE BACKFIELD FUNDAMENTALS
10	LINEBACKER KEY DRILLS	DE KEY DRILL / DE PURSUIT SLED	M & T PURSUIT SLED / M & T TECHNIQUES	SKELETON OFFENSE–DEFENSE	
10	LBs join other coaches *as assigned*	JV: OFF LINE DRILLS / JV: 7-MAN SLED	VAR: 7-MAN SLED / VAR: OFF LINE DRILLS		
10	Kirchenheiter observe & isolate	FULL LINE OFFENSE/DEFENSE		Coordinate use of LBs with Lake	
10	KICKING GAME				
	TEAMWORK (VARSITY)	JV–SOPH TEAMWORK		VARSITY TEAMWORK	
		RAIDERS	OFFENSE	RAIDERS	OFFENSE
45		DEFENSE	RAIDERS	DEFENSE	RAIDERS
	SPRINTING & CONDITIONING				

FIGURE 2-1

Daily Practice Schedule

2.   *Cross-Legged Toe Touch:* After a few touches, switch legs.
3.   *Straight from Squat:* Grasp ankles, lock-out knees, stretch the hamstrings and buttocks.
4.   *Knee Lift:* Leaning against wall, run in place with exaggerated high knee lift.

Specialty Period is as organized as can be without allowing it to become regimented. We feel that it sets a tempo for the rest of practice: if unsupervised, it leads to lax practices; if over-organized, it establishes an attitude of drudgery that is difficult to neutralize.

Calisthenics, like the weight lifting, are done quickly and aggressively. They are intended more to bring us together and speed up the tempo of practice than they are to warm us up. Each exercise is done for 10 to 12 seconds, as quickly as possible, jumping immediately into the next one. The sequence of exercises is as follows:

1.   Quick Jumping Jacks.
2.   Hit the deck for Push-Ups, as fast as possible.
3.   Flip over on your back for Quick-Sits (hands behind head, 60 percent raise).
4.   Raise up on head for Back (neck) Bridges (roll on hat).
5.   Jump up for Grass Drill (up, rt, lt, back).

Now repeat cycle of exercises 1 through 5.

6.   Pair off with partner for Neck Isometrics.
7.   Now close circle in on Captains for Quick Cal—Reaction Drills.

Movement from the large calisthenics group to small groups switches the responsibility for coaching to each staff member. While a general outline is presented here, it should be emphasized that each coach is free to coach his players as he sees fit. It is his responsibility to develop the drills, teaching progression and fundamental skills of his players. We simply ask that his timing be coordinated with the other coaches to facilitate best equipment utilization, that he include five minutes of Agility Drills on a daily basis, and that the basics of Attitude Tackling be incorporated into his drills.

ATTITUDE TACKLING

Regardless of the alignment, good defensive football depends on the player moving from his initial position into a collision course with the ballcarrier. We believe that the Invert Defense provides us with the best possible initial position for our players, and that our emphasis on agility, techniques and keys places them on the collision course. The important thing, then, is the tackler's attitude when he reaches the ballcarrier.

Check any game film, and count the number of form tackles made by your squad. Probably the most frustrating thing in coaching is to spend so much time teaching this aspect of the game, only to receive such a small return on the investment. It is not that we don't believe in the basic fundamentals that are requisites of good tackling—the breakdown position, eyes open, and movement into the ballcarrier on contact; we just don't accept the traditional Form Tackling Drills that have been common for so many years. We found very little correlation between a player's ability to square off in front of a standing or walking teammate, pick him up with his face in the numbers and walk him five yards, and the on-the-field ability to "stick-em." Instead of talking about form, we attempt to accentuate the development of an aggressive and confident self-image for the tackler by using a series of drills and teaching techniques designed to "psych" him into attacking the ballcarrier.

The drills are not limited to the field; as a matter of fact, some of the best image-building can be accomplished off the field and in off-season. The breakdown position is not only basic to good tackling; it is the ready position for essentially all athletic activities. When you meet a player in the halls after school, or practically anywhere or any time, and command "breakdown," or ask him how to guard his man in basketball or what stance a baseball shortstop uses, he should immediately react by breaking down. His understanding of the position's checkpoints, his readiness to assume it, and his desire to identify with it all contribute to his self-confidence.

One spring, as a part of our regular program of maintaining contact with our athletes during the off-season, we sent the note shown in Figure 2-2 to our players. The response was startling and immediate: "Coach, that was my brother you were talking about

WHY WON'T "HE" HIT

"He" has the ability to be a good football player. He is quick, has adequate size and has always been a fair athlete, but the fact of the matter is "he won't hit." In our freshman year, the coach picked him to be a starter, but after a few weeks he lost his job because he shied away from contact. He never won it back. I've always wondered, "Why won't he hit." I've got to admit, hitting someone head-on with your face doesn't sound like a pleasant experience. Why, I can remember when "he" and I played on the same Little League football team, and the coach said, "We're going to find out who the football players are," and lined us up ten yards apart, and we took turns running at each other. A couple of guys even got hurt that day; as a matter of fact, he was one of the guys that "had his bell rung" that time.

It is not like that anymore, however, because of the equipment and the maturity of the players. If you keep your head up and hit with the forehead of your helmet so that your neck is bulled, you can take your opponent right to the ground. Now, that is a pleasant feeling. Nothing could be more satisfying than a good "stick." It is like they say—you can hear the good ones, they never hurt, and best of all, everybody knows you did it.

I figured "he'd" quit football this year, but it looks as though he is going to hang in there. It is funny that the coaches don't pressure him too much. They sure don't take any extra time with him trying to teach him to "stick"; they just put him through the same basic drills that we go through. But then, what could they do special for him that they don't already do with us? The assistant coach in charge of our group has said a thousand times that blocking and tackling are simply a matter of combining some simple techniques, such as the "breakdown position," stepping into a man, keeping your eyes open and using your own natural strength. From there on, it is simply a matter of wanting to get the *good hit*. Our head coach says, "It only takes one good one to make a hitter." He tells of a boy that wasn't good enough to play regularly with the Junior Varsity for half a season, but one time in a JV game, he was all that stood between an opponent and the game-tying TD. He made that hit, and it was a good one; it must have been because everybody heard it. From that day on, he improved quickly, and the next year he was the *best* player in the league at his position.

Wouldn't it be something if all of a sudden this year "he" gets that feeling of confidence that changes him from being a "sitter" to a "hitter"! Weights help; I know they do for me. I feel much stronger than the others because I know that I can use my body to advantage. I'll bet after a summer on weights and a fair start at the proper techniques in the fall, "he" would also be a "hitter." No, probably not; he really hasn't shown that extra desire. He probably wouldn't work at it; he'd just go through the motions, doing just enough to be with the guys, but not that little extra. I guess that is what the difference is between a *winner* and a guy who likes to win. But—wouldn't it be something if he really did get after it, and "he" was the difference, the difference between our having a good team and having a CHAMPIONSHIP team!

A teammate

FIGURE 2-2

An Off-Season Note to Players

in that note, wasn't it?" . . . "You're right about only needing one good hit to make the difference, Coach; that is exactly what happened to me last year" . . . and there were many more. We are convinced that this one note did more to improve our tackling than five hours of form tackling could.

In game situations, a tackler must contend with a number of conflicting stimuli before attacking the ballcarrier. We include in our daily practice schedule two or three Hit-Reaction Drills, all of which are designed to simulate game situations under relatively safe conditions. The tackler must actively contend with interference while concentrating on the football. We try to vary the drills a little; our favorites are shown in Figures 2-3 through 2-5.

The approach completed, the true tackle begins when the tackler, with knees flexed, face up and arms spread, "tucks his tail," locks his arms and continues moving into the ballcarrier. This, however, is against human nature, and can only be accomplished "by accident." In the Butt Tackle Drill (Figure 2-6) we encourage the players to use their forearms or hands in the butt, until the third and final hit. They have to remove them to lock onto the ballcarrier, but it will become second nature to them to maintain the same position they have used in the previous butt, especially if they are being actively encouraged by their coach and teammates.

THE CAT DRILL

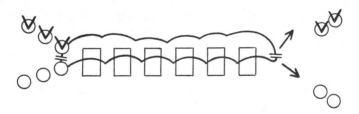

Coaching Points: Maintain low center of gravity (like a cat); keep shoulders parallel to line; maintain inside-out leverage on the ballcarrier; when he steps up—BUTT 'EM.

FIGURE 2-3

The Cat Drill

HIT-TRIANGLE

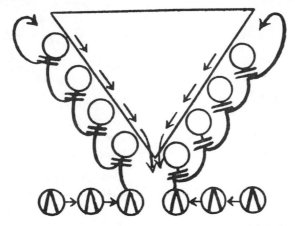

Coaching Points: This is a contain drill. The man attacking the triangle must work to establish contain on the ball by delivering blow with inside arm and moving up as well as laterally.

FIGURE 2-4

Hit-Triangle Drill

SHUCK DRILL

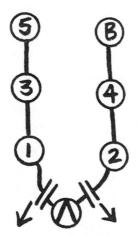

Coaching Points: Two lines alternately approach defender; as he "shucks" or knocks each off to their respective side, he sets for the other. Last man handles ball, BUTT 'EM.

FIGURE 2-5

Shuck Drill

BUTT TACKLING

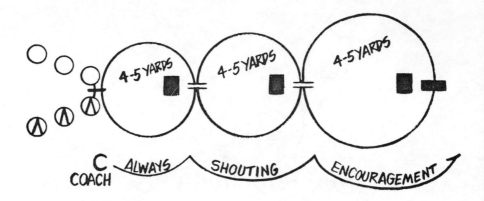

Coaching Points: Tackling is butting without the hands and arms for protection. On the first two butts, establish good hitting position; on the third, the tackler must bring his man down, and *if encouraged* by an enthusiastic coach who is moving along directly behind him, will do it by opening his arms, tucking his tail. Then it is a matter of FEET, FEET, FEET.

FIGURE 2-6

Butt Tackle Drill

For variety, two other tackling drills may be substituted for the Butt Tackle, but again, the purpose is more to establish a positive attitude toward tackling than it is to develop form.

BALANCE TACKLE DRILL

Coaching Points: Tackler runs at full speed, but as he approaches the ballcarrier he "chokes his motor," shortening his stride and widening his base. Runner steps up on one side of bag or other, and tackler BUTTS 'EM.

FIGURE 2-7

Balance Tackle Drill

GOAL LINE TACKLING

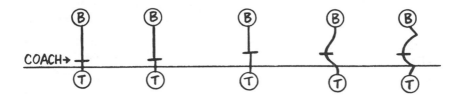

Coaching Points: One pair at a time. A simple challenge: "Don't let him score; be better, be tougher, WIN."

FIGURE 2-8

Goal Line Tackling

THE COACHES' LESSON PLAN

Good practices don't begin when the coach steps onto the field, nor are they the product of a neatly mimeographed schedule with blocks of time filled in. Instead, planning for well-organized practices begins soon after the close of the previous season. It is then that a staff is best able to sit down and objectively evaluate the strengths and weaknesses shown during the previous season. We like to divide the off-season into three large blocks of time.

The winter months are for review and evaluation. We'll consider what we have been doing, right or wrong, and how we can go about improving our program.

The spring is a time for learning. We attempt to have as many of our coaches as possible attend the various clinics, conferences and college spring practices available to us. We have found that informal gatherings at a coach's home can be very productive. It is quite easy to find area high school coaches, or college assistants who might be recruiting the area, to come and speak about some aspect of their program.

By late spring, we are ready to start putting the pieces together. With regard to our overall defense, all staff members will have had the opportunity to offer advice, and the Defensive Coordinator and Head Coach will cooperatively go about the task of rewriting the Defensive Manual. We are probably one of the few high schools in the nation whose Defensive Manual is more comprehensive than the Offensive. It is imperative, we feel, to rewrite this notebook every year for two basic reasons. Each year we find better ways of communicating our ideas to the players. By changing a phrase, rewording a technique or clarifying a responsibility, we might make it easier for one player to do a better job. If the entire thing is being rewritten, each coach is more willing to look for ways of improving it. Secondly, as you read through and revise things you have done in the past, you can't help but learn something new, in light of the experience you have gained during the year that just ended.

By summer, the manual complete and distributed to the coaching staff, we are prepared to enter the final phase of incorporating the defense into the practice plan. We ask each coach to prepare a clinic lecture to be given to the rest of the staff, other coaching staffs or the local Pop Warner Football League coaches. An attentive audience is usually easy to come by, and personal pride will be all the encouragement a staff member needs to prepare his talk on "Coaching the Secondary" or "Defensive End Drills," etc. This gives the coach the opportunity to organize the drills and teaching methods that he will be incorporating into our practices in the fall. He knows that his audience will not simply accept a "that's the way we've always done it" reason for teaching a particular idea, and he must really understand what he is coaching.

The notes used by the respective coaches in their presentations are collected, organized and duplicated for each coach's notebook. Any staff member, by looking at his notes, should be able to relate, in general, what his colleagues are doing.

THE DEFENSIVE CLASSROOM

Communicating the entire defensive concept to the players is no small task. Complicated by New Jersey's September 1 starting date for football practice, pre-school drills will vary in length from two to seven days. We found it impractical to go away to football camp for such a short period and began holding our pre-season camp in our own school, sleeping in the gym and eating in the school cafeteria. Encouraged by its success and several advantages over camps away from school, we continued holding it at school, even when time permitted us to go away. It is during this encampment that the bulk of our teaching is accomplished.

Our presentation is not at all unique. We combine large group lectures with smaller specialized groups and on-the-field instruction. The rate at which we add things is determined by the players' on-the-field response to those items that have already been presented. There is no sense in teaching a set of split-end adjustments to players who are having difficulty aligning properly to the basic calls. Our general sequence of building the defense for our squad is as follows:

1. Our Defensive Philosophy
2. Monster and Chuckles, our basic calls
3. Review of Techniques and Keys (small groups)
4. Forcing Unit Stunts and the Pyramid of Pass Defense (small groups)
5. Goal-Line and Short-Yardage Defense
6. The Hawk Defense (small groups)

Teaching is a continuous process, and we constantly remind our staff that "it matters not what you have taught; what is measured, is what was learned." Our defense is tested every Saturday afternoon in front of a stadium full of fans. At times, they can be severe in their judgment of the performance of a high school athlete, but that is what the young man is being prepared for, and it is each coach's responsibility to insure that the boy be as well prepared as possible.

A high school boy has only a limited amount of time and energy to devote to football. By complete preparation and meaningful communication, the coach can utilize that time to prepare the boy for being a part of the "best" defense.

3

Coaching the Down Linemen
in the Invert Defense

The down linemen, Mike and the two tackles, represent the nucleus of our Forcing Unit. As indicated by its title, we expect the Forcing Unit to be an aggressive and highly mobile front wall whose prime purpose is to force our opponent into mistakes.

SELECTING PERSONNEL

Physically, there is usually a significant difference in the appearance of the three players making up this coaching triad. The Mikeman, for example, is most often the smallest of the three, but by far the quickest. If we have more than one outstanding linebacker prospect in a class, we will often try to work one into playing at the Mike position. In this spot there is a particular advantage to being short; this is one of the very few places in all competitive athletics where lack of height might be considered an asset. The reason is a simple one, but it is a grass roots aspect of the Invert Defense. The Mikeman will be aligned head-on the center and "scooping" (we'll explain this technique later) to the right or left on 95 percent of the offensive plays. In order to be successful at this technique, the prime requisite is that you "remove the blocking surface from the offensive center." The shorter (quicker) you are, the greater your chance for success in this maneuver. In addition to the physical qualities, we look for Mikemen who tend to be high strung or emotional football players. Being located directly over the football has definite advantages to a boy with quick reaction time.

The tackles also have their differences. We have found that most of our opponents run right-handed; that is, they tend to place the physically stronger offensive linemen to their offensive right side. While there are several sound ideas incorporated in their decision, we must live with the fact that our defensive left tackle had better be the strongest boy on our squad or we're going to be in trouble. So there he is, if he can "move it." We want the strongest boy, but we can not sacrifice aggressive mobility to achieve this desire. Our defense is first and foremost an attacking one, and by "strength," we're talking about the strength exhibited by a player who is out creating mayhem, not one who is able to stand his ground while being assaulted.

The right tackle physically is a cross between the Mike and the left tackle; that is, he is generally a little bigger than the Mikeman, but will rival him in quickness and movement. He has to be a little better on his feet than the left tackle, but generally will not be expected to equal him in pure strength.

It can not be emphasized enough that quickness, agility and aggressiveness are the qualities we seek most in our down linemen. We have not yet been blessed with one of those high school phenomena who are 6'5", weigh 250 pounds, and possess a sprinter's speed, but if we ever are, I assure you he'll play defense. Considering the average football player, however, the one who turns out for your team and ours, the big ones will play offense and the tough ones will play defense. An average 240-pound tackle will not perform as well on our defensive line as an aggressive 190-pounder.

THE MIKEMAN—IN ON 50 PERCENT OF THE TACKLES

While in reality this is not a true statistic, it is the starting point we use in coaching the middle guards. It does have a valid basis, however, as indicated in Figure 3-1.

If our Mike is looping in the correct direction—and by pure chance, that should be 50 percent of the time—he should be able

FIGURE 3-1

Mikeman Scoops to Play 50 Percent of Time

to make the play unless the offensive guard double-teams him. Naturally, there are a lot of buts, ifs and counter plays that may contradict that statement, but the essential point is that if our Mikeman can avoid the center's block, he is going to create havoc for your offense, our offense, or any offense.

So, starting with a quick and emotional young man, we sell him on the idea that he can be the most important football player on our squad—if he can learn to avoid the block of the offensive center.

Stance and Alignment: A balanced 4-point stance is essential, because you will be scooping, right or left, on almost every down. It is important not to indicate the direction in which the Mikeman is moving, and naturally he should be able to go right and left with equal ease. The depth at which Mike aligns off the ball will vary with his ability, the center's ability and the game situation. The more experienced the player becomes, the greater advantage he can achieve in varying the depth of his alignment. The average is between two and three feet off the ball. Generally, the better (quicker) he is the closer he can move to the ball.

Scoop Techniques (Either Direction): MOVE, as you take a lateral step with the foot in the direction in which you are scooping; simultaneously reach with the opposite hand toward the moving foot, keeping your head low as you remove the blocking surface from the center. EXPLODE into the gap by pushing off the outside foot and bringing a forearm shiver from the floor with the inside arm and leg. REACT to what is happening in front of you (Figure 3-2). If the center is reaching for you, and the guard fires on the linebacker, destroy the center's head with the shiver, square off in the hole and slide along the line until the ballcarrier comes to you. Don't chase the QB as he hands off; wait for them to bring it to you. We want a lot of little losses, not a few big ones (Reaction #1). If the guard is doubling or down blocking on you (Reaction #2), fight him; split the double team or move across his head if possible. Reaction #3—if the guard is pulling opposite your slant, and the center is encouraging your movement, spin out and pursue laterally. If the guard is pulling in the slant direction (Reaction #4), "get in his pocket"; he'll bring you to the ball. Finally, if you read pass (Reaction #5), follow-through with your forearm shiver on the center, and continue working through him to the passer. Your only draw responsibility is to the side you are scooping.

Other than the scoop in either direction, the Mike is involved in only two other variations of defensive line play. On Mike or Gap calls, he is asked to align in the gap to which he would have looped and "blow it." Quite frankly, we don't think there is a whole lot of coaching involved in this technique. Either you get into that gap, crowd the ball, and on the snap "make something happen," or you don't. The only real coaching point we try to make is that the initial step should be with the outside foot. This is important because the first step exposes a blocking surface, and we don't want that surface exposed to the outside blocker. It is far more difficult for the center to turn you out than it would be for a guard to cave you in.

On the goal line, or in any of the 6-man line short-yardage calls, a third and final technique applies. The defensive guards are responsible for both center-guard seams. The distance that the ball is from the goal and the yardage needed on a single play determine how wide the guards play. On a 1-10 at the ten, they would shade the inside of the guards and pressure to the outside. With less than one yard to go, they would each align with a piece of the center, and squeeze low and hard on the ball.

We ask little of the Mikeman with regard to techniques; instead, emphasis is placed on developing his individual quickness, agility, movement and tackling attitude. The biggest coaching job with Mikemen deals with "pulling their reins." By that we mean

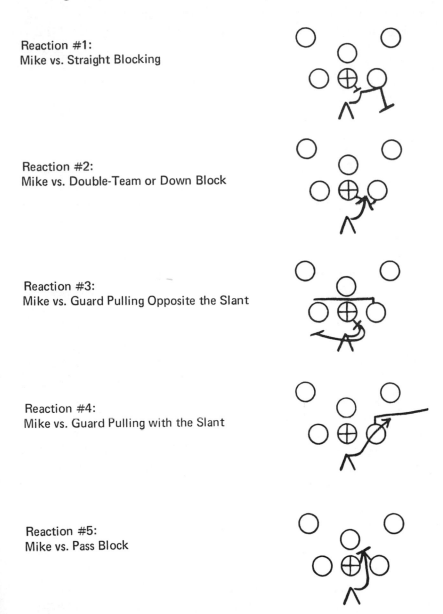

Reaction #1:
Mike vs. Straight Blocking

Reaction #2:
Mike vs. Double-Team or Down Block

Reaction #3:
Mike vs. Guard Pulling Opposite the Slant

Reaction #4:
Mike vs. Guard Pulling with the Slant

Reaction #5:
Mike vs. Pass Block

FIGURE 3-2

Mike's Scoop Reactions

bringing them under control with no more than one yard's penetration so that they can react to the blocking pattern. This is a delicate situation, as the Line Coach has been stirring the fires that drive them; yet we can not lose sight of the fact that ours is a *team* defense, and that play at every position is coordinated with the others.

THE LINE COACH, A DIFFICULT RESPONSIBILITY

Before moving on to the discussion of tackle techniques, it might be worth while to pause and examine the difficult task of coaching the linemen. The Line Coach is the only coach who has to work with a group not specifically offensively or defensively oriented. He is usually burdened with the largest number of players in any group, and often with some of the younger boys, a segment not athletically gifted. His job is to mold these boys into smaller sub-units that will be highly motivated to perform football's least rewarding tasks, offensive and defensive line play. In order to do this effectively, it is imperative that the Head Coach yield a great deal of authority to him to establish a close rapport with the linemen. He must learn whom to push and pressure, and who responds best to a kind word and a pat on the back. He must be willing to coach on the run, for if he tends to bog down in explanations and demonstrations, the boys who need running and quickness most will be deprived of it. Just as we must seek ways to bring recognition to linemen for their efforts, we must strive to recognize this coach and his players. They are the ones who can turn the tide of victory.

THE INSIDE LOOP

Our basic tackle techniques are called Inside and Outside Loops. The Inside Loop, used when the slant of the line is *away* from that particular tackle, is nothing more than the same scoop technique of the Mikeman. It is important, I suppose, to explain why we believe in this technique and do not play the standard slant tackle technique of the Arkansas Monster Defense. First, it must be remembered that we are as likely to slant our line into the shortside of the field as we are away from it. It is important that our interior lineman maintain sufficient body control to be able to fight back against an offensive tackle attempting to cave him in to the direction of his slant. Quite frankly, we don't think our high school football players are capable of doing as Coach Frank Broyles suggests: "Lining head-on the offensive tackle, slanting to the inside on a 45° angle, keying the guard while playing the offensive tackle with his hands."[1] Coach Broyles further suggests that "on plays his way, he must turn up field into the play—trying to get penetration and disrupt the play in the backfield." we have found that if a high school tackle is going to concern himself with handfighting the man he is lined up on, he is not going to slant down the line with any sincere interest in causing mayhem. We feel that the scoop technique, as previously outlined for Mikeman, gives us the best of area control and forcing activity, particularly when we offer the Blood stunt as an occasional alternative.

Stance and Alignment: Our tackle also plays from a 4-point stance, and is aligned on the outside eye of the offensive tackle. His depth, again, varies, and is determined by the relative quickness of the offensive tackle and himself. He can not allow either the Inside or Outside Loops to be cut off, and the closer he can be to the ball, still successfully completing his loops, the better. Generally, one to two feet back from the ball will suffice.

Loop Technique: Using the same technique as the Mike, the away tackle moves into the guard-tackle gap and "reads" the offensive guard and tackle. Against straight blocking, Reaction #1 of Figure 3-3, the tackle will occupy the dive hole and exert as much pressure as possible back toward the off-tackle area. Occasionally, he will have to spin-out if the tackle has been able to move him down the line. Another blocking scheme that we often see is the "fold block" (Reaction #2), where the guard blocks out on the tackle and the offensive tackle steps around the block and comes up the hole on the linebacker. Reacting to this from his scoop position, the tackle must attack the guard, neutralizing his charge, and clutter the inside running lane with both their bodies. If the guard blocks toward the Mikeman (Reaction #3), he reads it as a trap, lowers his inside arm to the ground, keeps square and

---

[1] Lecture by Frank Broyles, University of Arkansas, at Kutchters Country Club Football Clinic, June 28, 1967.

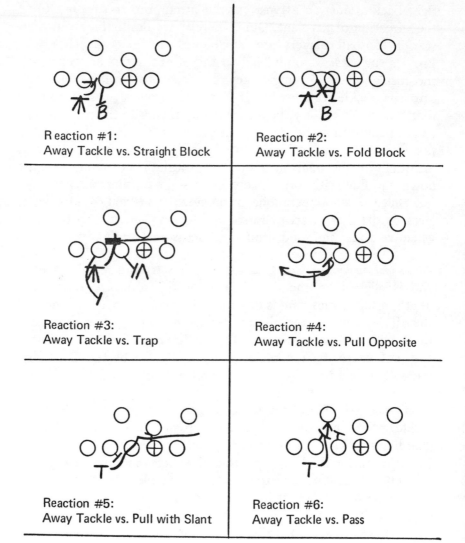

Reaction #1:
Away Tackle vs. Straight Block

Reaction #2:
Away Tackle vs. Fold Block

Reaction #3:
Away Tackle vs. Trap

Reaction #4:
Away Tackle vs. Pull Opposite

Reaction #5:
Away Tackle vs. Pull with Slant

Reaction #6:
Away Tackle vs. Pass

FIGURE 3-3

Away Tackle's Reactions

prepares to "knock the trapper back to where he came from." If
the guard is pulling behind the tackle (Reaction #4), we prefer to

spin out of the tackle's block rather than attempt to step around it, because we feel that we are still in front of the play and not trailing it as is often the case with the step-around. We pride ourselves on how well our away (scoop) tackle can get "into the hip pocket" of a guard pulling away from him (Reaction #5), while using a scoop technique. The crossing of the outside arm gives him a lever to push away from the seal block, encouraging his movement down the line with only slight penetration. The final reaction (#6) to the pass is the same as for the Mikeman: attack only one blocker, in this case the tackle. Check the draw to your side, and get after them.

THE OUTSIDE LOOP

The technique for the Outside Loop is different than the scooping done by the tackle on his inside maneuver. Unfortunately, it took us several years to recognize this fact, even though we had originally been taught the proper approach. When we were first introduced to the concept of Invert Defense by Bill Parcells, himself a tackle at the time, he cautioned that it was important for the tackle to deliver the blow on the tight end with his *inside arm*. After a short period of teaching it that way, we conceded that it was not practical and allowed the equivalent of the scoop technique to be used at all line positions. We hoped that it would simplify our teaching. Statistics after two seasons, however, showed us the error in our thinking. Our weakest area was off-tackle on the side of the loop, the place we expected would be the strongest. We discovered that by allowing our tackle to square off in the off-tackle hole, he was contained by the tight end's down block, creating a running lane (Figure 3-4) between himself and the loop end, who was susceptible to the kick-out block of a pulling guard.

Correcting this error was the most difficult coaching problem we had encountered with the Invert Defense. We ultimately resorted to the U.S. Army's "by the numbers" teaching method to accomplish the task. The Outside Loop, which is similar in technique to the pulling of an offensive guard on a short trap, was broken down into three distinct phases and taught "by the numbers":

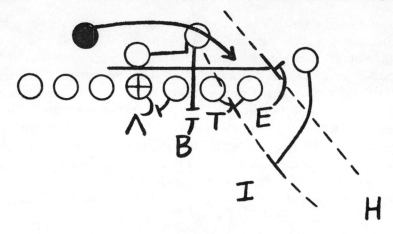

FIGURE 3-4

Running Lane Resulting from Improper Tackle Play

1. *The Jab:* Take a lateral step to the outside by throwing the outside elbow in the intended direction, dipping the shoulder to remove the blocking surface from the tackle and looking directly at the tight end.
2. *The Blow:* Now, while looking directly at the end, step up and deliver a blow with the inside arm and leg. If the end is blocking down or working as part of a double-team, contact will be made at this point. The outside arm and leg are free to "wipe off" the end and gain control of the area.
3. *The Square-Off:* If the end is not blocking down, your position will force his outside release, keeping him from the linebackers, and you can simply follow through with the final steps—a squaring of the shoulders and feet at the line of scrimmage.

Again, we try to acquaint the tackle with the kind of blocking patterns he might see as he completes his loop so that he is more comfortable in handling them. The variety outside is less, but the difficulty in handling each is far greater. In Figure 3-5, the reactions for most common blocking patterns are shown. In Reaction #1, a straight block, the tackle occupies the off-tackle

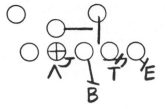

Reaction #1:
Loop Tackle vs. Straight Blocking

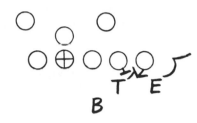

Reaction #2:
Loop Tackle vs. Double-Team

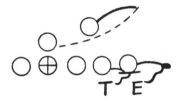

Reaction #3:
Loop Tackle vs. Reach Block

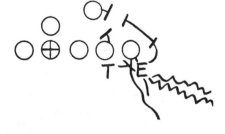

Reaction #4:
Loop Tackle vs. Pass Block

FIGURE 3-5

Loop Tackle Reactions

hole and fights back to close the dive hole. Occasionally, a spin-out (in) would be desirable. The most important play, of course, is beating the double team (Reaction #2). The technique, explained in the "by the numbers" discussion, emphasizes the blow by the inside arm and the wipe-off. Reaction #3 is simply a pair of reach blocks, a situation where the advantage is clearly to the loop tackle, and simply requires running through the block. Finally, Reaction #4, to a pass, is our most unusual one; it will be discussed in further detail.

A UNIQUE ROLE IN PASS DEFENSE

In its original form (Figure 3-6), our defense was excellent against the run and gave outstanding secondary play, but our pass rush left much to be desired, particularly on the side of the loop.

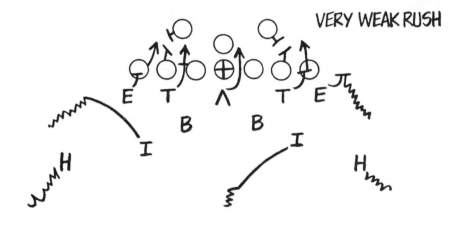

FIGURE 3-6

Original Line Play vs. Pass

Similarly, on sprint-out action toward the loop, our coverage was excellent, but we had a difficult time containing the passer. The loop tackle would get involved on the line of scrimmage, and could not establish a quick contain on the passer (Figure 3-7).

We contemplated several changes that might compensate for this weakness, but it kept coming back to involving the tackle in pass coverage, unacceptable by all traditional standards. Then, while reading the Proceedings of the American Football Coaches Meeting, January, 1969, we came across the following statement by Marty Hopkins, Centerville Community College,[2] in an article on "The Centerville College Monster Defense":

> . . . We give our off-side tackle one other responsibility that on paper looks extremely hard to execute, but in actual practice comes easily to a tackle using a loop technique. We ask him to cover the flat on his side when he reads dropback pass. We do this first because we don't want the end worrying about whether or not to rush or cover the flat, and second because we don't feel a tackle whose first responsibility is to hit and occupy the offensive end's outside is going to be able to put on a very effective rush.

That was the clincher. We reviewed our responsibilities, and made the change in flat responsibility for the upcoming season. We have been extremely pleased with the success of this maneuver, and although we retained a "switch" call that permitted us to

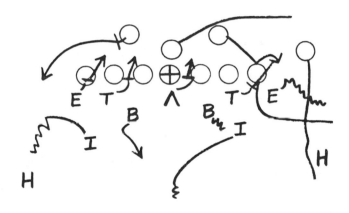

FIGURE 3-7

Original Line Play vs. Sprint-out

revert back to the older system, we have had to incorporate it only once in three seasons. While the tackle may not be the best pass defender, the improved pass rush from the defensive end and the

---

[2]Marty Hopkins—Ted Heath, "The Centerville College Monster Defense," Proceedings of the Forty-sixth Annual Meeting, American Football Coaches Association (January 7, 8, 9, 1969), p. 74.

inability of the offense to guess when the tackle will be covering the flat have made this a great asset to our overall defensive scheme.

As the tackle steps up to deliver the blow on the tight end, we ask him to ride him into the flat if he "feels pass." If he has already squared off in the hole before recognizing, we want him to retreat to the flat the same as a linebacker does in going back to the hook zone. If there was only one receiver to his side, the end, he will concentrate on picking up the second receiver coming out of the backfield. This aspect alone has significantly improved our coverages of screen passses so often thrown into the short side

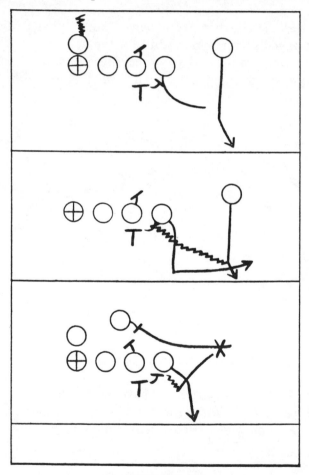

FIGURE 3-8

Loop Tackle's Pass Coverage

opposite the wing. The plays in Figure 3-8 show the loop tackle's typical pass coverage responsibilities.

OTHER TACKLE TECHNIQUES

Like those of the Mikeman, the techniques to be learned by the tackles other than the basic loops are simple and used only with stunts and change-offs. The Blood charge is exactly what it sounds like. We tell the tackle that he, along with the end, can simply put his ears back and slant down to the inside on a 45° angle across the butt of the next man inside. Their play is not complicated by handfighting with the tackle; they are simply expected to get into the backfield and "make something happen!"

On Away and Gap calls, the tackle, like the Mike, will align in his assigned gap and "blow it." As with the Mikes, the only important coaching point is that the initial step be taken with the outside foot.

If an Outside Loop is called for, but there is no one to loop on to because the tight end or slotback has split in excess of two yards, we use what we call a Spy technique. The end with a nasty split has limited his ability to block back effectively on the tackle. With that potential reduced, the Spy technique is most effective. The tackle merely loops just enough to assure outside position on the offensive tackle and a clear vision of the near setback. This gives him a better opportunity to squeeze down on inside running plays, aiding the control of the inside area by the linebacker and Mikeman without reducing his ability to fulfill his own responsibilities.

On the goal line, the only real change is that we ask the tackles to "flatten their loops." By referring to it in this manner, the goal line charge is still related to the tackle's normal defensive play, with special emphasis on getting to the point of attack a little quicker. Also, the loop tackle is relieved of his flat responsibility. The entire goal line defensive scheme will be explained more completely in Chapter 8.

COMMON DENOMINATORS FOR GOOD DEFENSIVE LINE PLAY

Keys: In addition to the factors that relate to the specific techniques and responsibilities of each position, there are several factors that contribute to good line play that must be communicated to the athletes. "Keys," for example, are the door openers. They are what you need to know to get moving on the snap of the ball. For all defensive linemen, their key is the same—the hand of their closest opponent. Before any lineman moves out of his stance, the first thing he'll do is "pick up the anchor." We want our linemen concentrating on this movement so they can initiate their own movement as quickly as possible.

Beating the Double-Team: This is one of the fundamentals that we have complicated by looping and scooping in the line. The Line Coach would prefer to say we split it, or we drop down and grab grass, or we spin out or whatever, as long as there was a single method to drill for it, but that is not the case. If you are looping into the drive man of a double team, your outside arm should be free, and you beat the double team by beating that man only. On a scoop, it is usually more practical to split the double-team, or slide across the drive blocker's face, if possible. If you have turned your back on the drive blocker, as you might if looping or scooping away from him, then the spin-out is the only practical method to use. Beating the double-team is best accomplished by a boy who understands the blocking scheme he sees developing in front of him.

Pass Rush: While there are many techniques for good pass rush available, we felt that we should limit our teaching to one method and depend on the physical ability of our athletes to carry us beyond that point. Besides, we don't have time to teach more than one method. We like to teach the "hit and swim" technique. When the lineman has come under control with a penetration of up to one yard, and reads "pass," he attacks one opposing blocker (normally the one he lined up on) and delivers a blow. Reaching across with the free arm he tries to swim (pull) past the blocker. He shouldn't try to keep running through him; instead, he should try to knock him off balance and move past him.

Spin-out: We have stated several times that we encourage the spin-out rather than a step-around technique when trying to reverse direction. If you have looped or scooped properly, the blocker controlling you is on your side or back. By leaning into him, pivoting on the near foot and throwing the arm away from him around, you can use his body as the pivot point for the spin and move around him quickly, arriving in a good football position and ready to move into the ball.

Faking a Loop: After you have gained confidence in the starting count being used by your opponent, it sometimes is beneficial to give him a fake loop: that is, start your move in the wrong direction, recover, and be prepared to loop correctly on the snap. This should only be done occasionally, perhaps twice a game, or it will lose its intended effectiveness.

Talk to Each Other: Nothing can be more upsetting to a guard preparing to trap than to hear his opponent caution his teammate, "Watch the trap," "Check the double-team," etc. We want our linemen to look for tip-offs from the opponent, especially when preparing for the game. We caution the players to "look for tip-offs, but play your correct responsibility first; ours is a *team* defense."

Nothing has been said about pursuit as yet, but it should be emphasized that our team pursuit is our strongest asset. The techniques and coaching points applicable to our concept of pursuit will be explained in Chapter 5.

LINE DRILLS

Defensive line play, for drilling purposes, can be broken down into the following categories:

1. Stance and Movement
2. Reaction to Blocking Pattern
3. Beating the Blocker
4. Pursuit and Tackling

A glance back at our daily practice schedule (Figure 2-1) reveals that the principal elements of the above four categories are provided for in the lineman's practice schedule. Agilities and Hit-Reaction Drills are the principal methods of improving the defender's ability to whip the blocker, move to the ball and do something when he gets there. The Pursuit Sled Drills will be explained later, but you can see they are a regular part of the practice schedule. Stance and movement are provided for on a daily basis with a regularly scheduled period for Mike and tackle techniques. Finally, reacting to the blocking pattern is incorporated in the Full Line Offense/Defense period. A few of the drills that we feel are most important are outlined in the following pages.

JAB DRILL (Figure 3-9)

Purpose: To develop quickness and proper lateral movement in the initial step of both the scoop and loop techniques.
Procedure: On visual signal, the front men of three lines take initial step of scoop (loop) charge, then return to proper stance to repeat several times before being replaced by next man in line.
Coaching Points: Removal of blocking surface, eyes up to read.

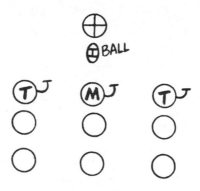

FIGURE 3-9

LOOP (SCOOP) BY THE NUMBERS

Purpose: To insure that each lineman understands the three parts of each charge.
Procedure: Same lines as Jab Drill; now follow through the three parts of the charge, pausing at each to review the coaching points.
Coaching Points: These are explained in the description of each charge.

LOOP AND PURSUE

Purpose: To insure that linemen come under control with no more than one yard of penetration.
Procedure: Same lines, loop and scoop in given direction, then react to visual signal to pursue in either direction.

Coaching Points: Be sure that good loop and scoop techniques are not forgotten when another assignment is added. Keep the lines of pursuit *flat* along the line.

OUTSIDE LOOP, 2-ON-1 DRILL (Figure 3-10)

Purpose: Develop skill and experience in handling the double-team block. Recognition of blocking patterns.
Procedure: Tight end and tackle double-team tackle making outside loop.
Coaching Points: Be sure that tackle is moving low and that he faces into the tight end, so that he can "wipe him off" with the outside arm.

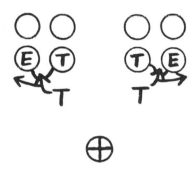

FIGURE 3-10

SCOOP, 2-ON-1 DRILL

Purpose and Procedure: Same as above.
Coaching Points: Check for definite lateral movement, removal of blocking surface and good explosion. Build slowly on the various blocking patterns to be seen. Have good execution against each one before moving to the next.

PASS RUSH DRILL

Purpose: To build on the skills involved with rushing the passer.
Procedure: Working out of two lines, scooping to the right or left, they rush first toward a drop-back pass position, and then toward positions applicable for the release points for roll-out passes.
Coaching Points: Attack one blocker, neutralize him with shiver from closest arm and use the free arm to swim, pull or knock him away.

4

Coaching the Invert Defense's
Ends and Linebackers

Every defense places particular demands on the quality of players at each position, but in most instances, as it is with the Invert Defense, the real football players must be located at the linebacking and defensive end positions.

FOUR "FOOTBALL PLAYERS" NEEDED

"He is a real football player" is a compliment reserved for only the most deserving players on your squad. We feel that a linebacker or a defensive end must possess the skills, attitudes and knowledge implied in that compliment in order to make our defense function successfully. Certainly there are a lot of boys, quite different in appearance and personality, who have been paid that honor, but they all have several traits in common that make them better players.

Mental toughness most certainly would head our list of attributes desired for these positions. The boy with a deeply engrained desire to compete, to achieve and to win is the kind of athlete we are looking for. His aggressive attitude may be masked with a shield of humility, and we hope it is, but when the whistle blows he will be ready to play, whether it is in front of a big crowd or on the practice field.

Of all the physical traits, we consider *quick feet* to be the most important. By "quick feet," we mean that the player possesses quickness and agility while working in a confined situation. Comparing the time it takes a boy to react to a visual stimulus, hit the deck, rise and re-establish a good football position is as good a single test for potential ends and linebackers as any we know.

Good *upper body strength* is a second physical qualification that must be seriously considered because it is necessary to keep blockers off their legs, while concentrating past the intended blocker to the ballcarrier. While pure running speed is not always a good indicator, it is necessary that ends, and particularly linebackers, have good range or lateral movement as well as quick acceleration into the contact area. We have found it practical to utilize left-handers on the right side whenever available. A "lefty" tends to use his left arm and foot better in delivering a blow, and in moving laterally to the outside from that position.

To continue listing traits we consider important would merely be a rehash of lists we have all seen before. Let it suffice to say that our defensive ends and linebackers are *good athletes* and, more importantly, they are *winners*.

DEFENSIVE END PLAY

The physical demands of playing defensive end are equalled by the mental demand for concentration and consistency. Understanding one's responsibilities and following them through will more than compensate, in the long run, for the big loss achieved by playing a hunch or taking a chance. A few seasons ago we had the finest pair of ends in our history. One was a crowd pleaser; when he made a "hit," everyone in the ball park knew it. He intimidated people with his physical prowess, but frustrated the staff with mental errors. His counterpart was steady and effective, and proved to be twice as effective on our defensive charts.

The techniques and reactions required of our defensive ends have been carefully analyzed and reviewed. They have been selected because they can be taught in a meaningful manner and improved with hard practice. We feel that they work best within the framework of our *team* defensive concept.

Stance and Alignment: The end assumes a 2-point stance, inside foot forward with the inside arm protecting that knee. We like our ends to get their feet just slightly closer than is really comfortable, so that when they step up on their anchor move, for example, they are stepping into a more comfortable and more natural stance than they had to start with. Otherwise, they would be moving out of a balanced, comfortable stance into an extended, less favorable hitting position. The inside foot should be aligned on the outside ear of the tight end, crowding the ball as much as possible. Since the first step will be with the up foot in both Anchor and Loop techniques, the player's weight should be settled just slightly back on the rear foot. His key for initial movement, again, is the down hand of the tight end. *Attack* when he "picks up anchor."

Anchor Technique: When the line slant is away from an end, his responsibility is to anchor the backside. His technique is to step forward with his inside (up) foot and deliver a blow, neutralizing the offensive end, closing the off-tackle area, and reacting to the attempted block of the tight end. As it was for the linemen, the basic blocking patterns have been identified and a set of reactions established. We work against the various blocks each day in the Key Drill, which we will outline later. The Blood stunt is a variation of the Anchor technique for which details were given in the description of the tackle's play. The same coaching points apply to the defensive end.

Loop Technique: With the exchange of responsibilities that has the loop tackle covering the flat on passes, the loop end's play was made considerably easier, and consequently our overall defense was more effective. From the same stance and alignment used when anchoring, except that he might wish to cheat back slightly off the ball, the end crosses over with his front leg on the movement of the tight end's hand. He quickly squares up with his outside foot and establishes immediate contain on the football. If he encounters an immediate blocking threat to his outside, such as a tight wingback, he'll attack him during the initial movement. If he is concerned with a potential crackback block of a wing split several yards, he can immediately turn to the inside, showing his back, a clipping surface, to the outside blocker. We prefer, however, that he concentrate on keeping his inside foot forward whenever possible, allowing him to better contend with a kickout block and permitting quicker lateral movement to the outside when his containment is threatened. On the snap he must look through to the closest back as his most immediate threat.

Pass Rush: From both Anchor and Loop movements, pass rush responsibilities for the end are the same *after* the initial play at the line. We ask that the end attack the QB through the near setback. Quite often, he'll recognize an attempted screen pass, and, by first hitting the back, have time to move with him. Also, by consistently going through this near back, the passer is confined to the pocket, reducing his chances to scramble and turn a poor play into a big one.

Anchor End Key Drill: The Key Drill for ends (Figure 4-1) is a regular part of our daily practice schedule. In the beginning, we'll work on a single situation in each practice, providing the opportunity for the end to fully understand his responsibility. Later, we combine several threats in the same drill to develop his play recognition. Beginning with an anchor end moving to attack the tight end with his inside flipper, we read his head. Reaction #1, to a reach or hook block, is to attack the blocker's head, get depth and force the play deep. Then begin to pursue along the line of scrimmage. If the end fires at you, attempting to turn you out, Reaction #2, fight to a stalemate, closing, if possible, the off-tackle hole. If the end turns down toward the tackle, and you are not immediately threatened by a wingback, Reaction #3, shuffle to close inside, keeping the inside foot up and protected. Against a double-team, or a double down block, Reaction #4, attempt to split it. It is important that you hold your ground, establishing as wide a corner as possible. Knock the end off stride if he is trying to release inside, Reaction #5, and similarly, if he wants an outside release, Reaction #6, force him to release flatter than he wishes, and immediately establish your pass rush route.

Loop End Reactions: The loop end sees the same initial movements (Figure 4-2) as the anchor end, but his position has been moved to one of immediate contain and his attention must quickly change to the action of the near setback (or wing). The offensive end should have no chance to contain him with a reach block,

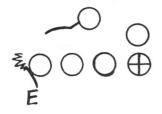

Reaction #1:
Anchor End vs. Hook Block

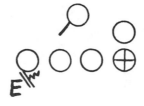

Reaction #2:
Anchor End vs. Turn-Out Block

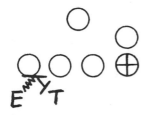

Reaction #3:
Anchor End vs. Down Block

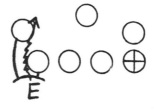

Reaction #4:
Anchor End vs. Double-Team

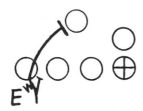

Reaction #5:
Anchor End vs. Inside Release

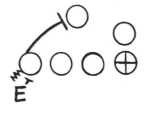

Reaction #6:
Anchor End vs. Outside Release

FIGURE 4-1

Anchor End's Key Reactions

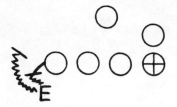

Reaction #1:
Loop End vs. Reach Block

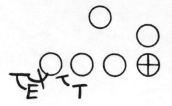

Reaction #2:
Loop End vs. Turn-Out Block

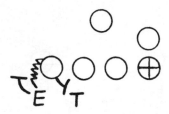

Reaction #3:
Loop End vs. Down Block

Reaction #4:
Loop End vs. Double-Team

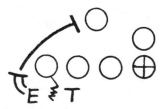

Reaction #5:
Loop End vs. Inside Release

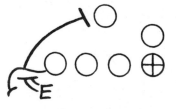

Reaction #6:
Loop End vs. Outside Release

FIGURE 4-2

Loop End's Key Reactions

Reaction #1, and he can readily get depth to contain the football. His initial movement has, of course, made a turn-out block, Reaction #2, already successful, but the loop tackle is in ideal position to defend the off-tackle area. The end's responsibility would continue to be one of containment. A down block on the tackle by the tight end, Reaction #3, isolates the end. Upon recognition, he must stop penetration, protect his outside leg and reduce the running lane, while maintaining his ability to pursue flatly to the outside. Against the end-wingback combination, Reaction #4, the loop end must emphasize his attack on the wing to successfully maintain a contain position. Against the end's inside release, Reaction #5, full responsibility for delaying action belongs to the tackle. The end is free to pressure the passer through the near setback. On an outside release, Reaction #6, the loop end has a fine opportunity to delay the receiver while establishing his pass rush lane.

Whether the end is looping or anchoring, on action away from him his responsibility is the same: "Search and pursue." The path to be followed will vary slightly with the play, as occasionally there may be an opportunity to catch a play from behind by chasing it, but more often than not we encourage a path like the one shown in Figure 4-3, in which the end comes under control, "searches" for the bootleg and reverse threat, and when convinced it does not exist, establishes a good pursuit angle.

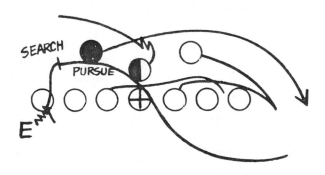

FIGURE 4-3

Defensive End's "Search and Pursue" Path

Formation Adjustments: The basic play of the ends described in the Anchor and Loop techniques is varied slightly in order to compensate for some formation variations. One that we see most often in high school football is the tight wingback. When looping toward a tight wingback, we emphasize that our end should attack him "face-up"so that he will not be hooked by the wing's block. We tell our anchor end just to be conscious of his presence, so that he can fight him as part of a double-team if and when it occurs.

The end with a "nasty split," defined as a split of two to five yards, is our next special case. We ask our end, whether looping or anchoring, to align on the offensive end's nose, crowding the ball. Attack him before he can attack you, and you will have more than offset any advantage he might have gained. The end must be aware of the tackle's loop, for if it was away from him he must be better prepared to close down, while if the loop is to him and the split is in excess of two yards, he'll probably call for a switch with the tackle and, after punishing the end, soften up and cover the flat, as the tackle has good contain potential from his position.

Any one of the varied "slot" alignments constitutes the third major formation that must be contended with. From the end's point of view, he simply considers the slotback a tight end and the split end a flanker. His alignment is on the slot and he'll play him as he would a tight end if he is close to the tackle. As the slot's position widens from the tackle, the defensive end must consider him to be more like a nasty end, and defend him accordingly. If it is a very tight slot, a loop end will have more success by moving across hard on the outside shoulder of the wing, presenting little or no crackback potential to the split end.

Adjustments made to a true split end have already been discussed in Chapter 1, as they involve several players and must be considered by the entire forcing unit. Drills for the ends are basically the same as for our other linemen, except that attention is given daily to the Key Drills in which the reactions previously outlined are practiced. Additional drills used for the ends will be discussed at the end of this chapter.

LINEBACKER TECHNIQUE AND RESPONSIBILITY

Because linebackers are usually such good football players, there is a tendency for coaches to let them rely on instinct to get to the football. We feel strongly that linebackers have to be coached more strictly than others in keying and proper technique. Some of our colleagues have had success flip-flopping their linebackers when playing behind a slanting line, so that they always have the same relationship with the slanting linemen in front of them. We have found that linebackers tend to perform better from one side of the formation, and adjust better to learning scrape and shuffle technique behind slanting tackles than they do when asked to play on the left on one play, and on the right on another. In addition, with our line generally not declaring its slant, switching the linebackers would be a key to the offense.

Stance and Alignment: Our linebackers are aligned in a breakdown position with the inside foot forward and pointing at the outside ear of the offensive guard. The depth must be sufficient to clear the defensive tackle's feet on a scrape reaction, and will also vary with down and distance, type of blocker at the guard and the major threats presented by the offensive style of play. If our linebacker is likely to overpower a smaller offensive guard, he will crowd him. If, however, the guard is bigger and stronger than himself, he'll back off more, forcing the guard to come up and out before reaching him. Placing the inside foot forward, at least toe to heel, is important to us because it forces a guard to extend himself across the front of the linebacker when trying to establish contact while blocking for an onside play.

Keys: Linebacker keys will vary from week to week depending on the findings of our scouting report, but to start with, our basic keys are the near setback for the linebacker on the side of the loop, and the QB for the away linebacker. We also insist that when keying backs, the key be read *through* the offensive guard. This means a linebacker can recognize a guard pull while actually keying in the backfield. The keys provide the linebacker with one of three basic reads, Scrape, Counter and Hook.

Scrape Reaction: This is the onside reaction; that is, the key is moving anywhere on the linebacker's side of the center. The most important aspect of the reaction is that the linebacker step across with his inside foot, simultaneously delivering a blow with his inside arm across the head of the offensive guard to turn that guard's body down along the line of scrimmage, "steering" his power along the line. Now he steps up with his outside leg to establish a "shoulders parallel" position, with the guard's body still occupying the original position and the linebacker up close, scraping along the line. If the tackle's loop was out, he is in the dive hold and will shuffle from there. If the tackle had looped in, he'll be filling immediately to his outside. Some boys find it difficult to take the first step with the inside foot; if this is the case, we will allow a slight shuffle outside, if it can be accomplished without giving too much depth.

A coaching technique we use to show our players how effective this scrape technique can be is to take a sophomore linebacker, allow him to turn the head of our best blocker, and then invite the blocker to attempt to drive him. If the head is turned, the blocker's body will follow it, and someone of lesser strength can steer a considerably bigger blocker. We spend a significant amount of time coaching our linebackers to turn their opponents down the line.

Counter Reaction: Of all our techniques, this one has been subjected to the greatest amount of experimentation. Originally, we asked the linebacker to shuffle one step to his own outside when reacting to a key that moved away from him. This worked fine in drills, but in the heat of a game a good football player does not move in the opposite direction from the ball without a great deal of discipline. After trying several alternatives, we have settled on what we feel is the best solution. When the key goes away, the linebacker steps up into the line with his inside foot and arm. If it is a straight play away from him, he is neutralizing the guard's block and is in position to pursue quickly. If a counter play is developing, this maneuver has held him on the backside long enough to read it, and puts him in a favorable position to contend with it. If the guard is pulling away, he'll sense it immediately and be able to quickly establish a deep pursuit path. Counter plays can be very effective against a team with a rich tradition of gang-tackling and relentless pursuit. Our linebackers must be well disciplined to fulfill their *team* defensive responsibility first.

Hook Reaction: The third and final linebacker "read" is pass. Initial pass responsibility on drop-back and semi-roll, when the corner is not threatened, is to cover the hook area to their side. This is best accomplished by crossing over with the inside leg and retreating on a 45° angle, while keying the quarterback and focusing on the inside receiver. We feel that we have developed the science of linebacker involvement in pass defense to a higher degree than most high school football teams. We spend a good deal more time teaching this aspect of pass defense because we believe that it is the short pass that develops into a long gain—not the bomb, that can spell upset to an otherwise sound defense. We refer to our linebacker's full pass responsibility as covering "hook to curl."

OUR UNDERCOVERAGE PHILOSOPHY: HOOK TO CURL

As the linebacker begins his drop to the hook area, he must pick up the tight receiver in his peripheral vision. His first responsibility is to prevent this tight receiver from running a crossing pattern by physically blocking his path. If this tight receiver (let's consider him a tight end) continues to run a straight pattern, he and the linebacker should run a collision course at about nine to ten yards down field. As the linebacker approaches that point, he'll ready to square off and shuffle in front of the potential hook threat. If, as is often the case, the inside receiver breaks off an outside cut before arriving at the hook area, the linebacker shifts into high gear and breaks for the curl point of the wide receiver.

We have found the curl pattern diagrammed in Reaction #3 of Figure 4-4 to be the best pass pattern in high school football—because linebackers are not adequately drilled in their role in defensing it. If linebackers can adequately defend the hook-to-curl area, passers are forced to resort to less consistent, poorer percentage pass patterns, the patterns that result in interceptions and curtailed drives.

On sprint action, when the corner is being challenged the linebacker's initial reaction is to the run, and one scrapes while the other counters. As the passer softens up and sets to pass, the backside linebacker will push back on his deep pursuit path and attempt to back into the seam away from the passer's flow. The scrape linebacker, unless he has found an immediate lane to the passer, will veer back, mirroring the depth of the passer, checking

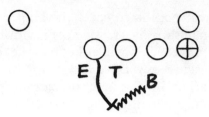

Reaction #1:
Preventing Crossing Pattern

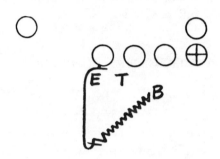

Reaction #2:
Defending the Hook

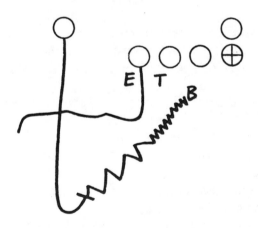

Reaction #3:
Defending the Curl

FIGURE 4-4

Linebacker Pass Coverage

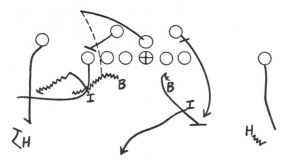

FIGURE 4-5

Sprint Action Pass Coverage

for a delayed release by a pass-blocking receiver and fronting the passer's running lane. Figure 4-5 shows the linebacker and secondary coverage to a sprint action pass.

On bootleg action passes, communication is the keynote to successful pass coverage by the linebackers. The key receiver is the tight end dragging with the quarterback opposite the initial flow. The linebacker, initially scraping, can not often prevent the tight end's cross, but he usually recognizes it. He calls to the other linebacker, "Push, push," hoping that the linebacker who is countering will be able to deepen and quickly focus on this crossing threat, eliminating the "drag end," the bootleg pass's principal receiver (Figure 4-6).

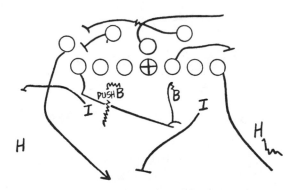

FIGURE 4-6

Linebacker Play vs. Bootleg Pass

Pass defense is worked into each linebacker's practice schedule. The drills, if you wish to call them that, are actually isolated segments of the Pass Reactions outlined in the preceding pages.

DEVELOPING LINEBACKERS WITH DRILLS

Our linebacker drills consist of three distinct phases. First, there are the Agility and Hit-Reaction Drills which have been discussed earlier as they related to Attitude Tackling (Chapter 2). These are concerned with the individual development of the football player and are equally applicable to defensive ends and others. The second phase concerns the development of specific skills necessary for playing the linebacking posts. We use a sequence of three drills for this purpose: Footwork Drill, the Neutralizer and Hit and React (Figures 4-7 — 4-9). Added to these will be some phase of the hook-to-curl pass coverage concept. Finally, the linebacker is added to either the full-line defense or the skeleton defense where his reactions are coordinated with those of his teammates.

The basic linebacker sequence of drills is simply a breakdown of his basic movements and key reactions.

FOOTWORK DRILL (Figure 4-7)

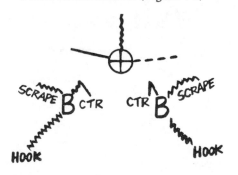

FIGURE 4-7

Purpose: To develop proper footwork used in basic key reactions.
Procedure: Coach, acting as the key, moves, indicating scrape, counter or hook.
Coaching Points: Good balance, good foot movement.

THE NEUTRALIZER (Figure 4-8)

FIGURE 4-8

Purpose: To develop the blow and coordinate movement paramount in the scrape reaction.
Procedure: Offensive guards fire out at the outside leg of linebacker, while linebacker "scrapes off."
Coaching Point: We have found it desirable to use those little one-arm shields on the inside arm of linebackers. It helps remind them of the use of that flipper, and our guards' heads are not punished unneccessarily.

HIT AND REACT (Figure 4-9)

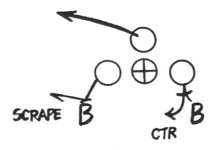

FIGURE 4-9

Purpose and Procedure: Combine the above drills into one. Develop good footwork and movement from initial blocker.
Coaching Points: Have guards block a play, so that one LB is reacting (scrape), while the other is "countering."

OTHER IMPORTANT DRILLS FOR LINEBACKERS AND ENDS

While the aforementioned linebacker and end Key Drills make up most of our practice schedule, we try to add variety to our daily practices to prevent boredom. On any given day, we might substitute five minutes of rope drills, using the suspended rope maze that is usually dominated by our offensive backs. The Pursuit Sled Drills, scheduled regularly for the ends, are included for linebackers at least twice each week.

The Contain Drill is one that is often included in the end's workout, while 2-on-1 Butt Drill is one of our favorite linebacker drills, occasionally substituted in the schedule.

CONTAIN DRILL (Figure 4-10

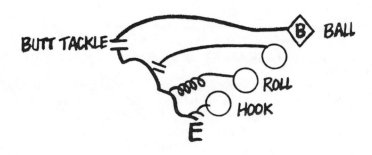

FIGURE 4-10

Purpose: To confront the ends with all of the blocking threats they might encounter while maintaining containment on the ball.
Procedure: First, the tight end attempts to hook him, followed by a roll-blocking guard, power-driving full back, and finally the ball. All this while, he is protecting his legs and keeping contain.
Coaching Points: Foot movement, use of hands and protection of outside leg.

2-ON-1 BUTT DRILL (Figure 4-11)

FIGURE 4-11

Purpose: To develop simultaneous arm and leg movement when delivering a blow.

Procedure: Coach stands behind linebacker who alternately shuffles back and forth between two offensive blockers. As he approaches, they step up to meet his blow.

Coaching Points: The blow is delivered with the inside arm, the outside hand being used to "wipe off" the blocker. Maintain good football position throughout drill, emphasizing the low center of gravity—"Keep your butt down."

5

Coordinating the Forcing Unit in the Invert Defense

To be considered a craftsman in his trade, a man must be able to produce a quality finished product from the available raw materials. The Invert Defense, we feel, provides the framework for a sound forcing unit, yet it is of little consequence unless it is properly incorporated into a meaningful game plan.

A SCHEDULE FOR DEFENSIVE PLANNING

There aren't enough hours in the day or days in the year to allow for the kind of preparation we all say we would like to do. But if it is to be effective, preparation must begin for next year immediately following the game with that particular opponent. While the problems are still fresh in your mind, you should make notes concerning any adjustments made on the field, ideas that are considered and possible areas of revision for the coming season. A particularly good idea, we have found, is to make a tape recording right after the game of your random thoughts and of any applicable thoughts that arise during the film review. A tape requires very little effort and can be easily put to service during the off-season.

Your scouting system and film exchange program, if allowed, require considerable planning to make them effective. Scouting for the Invert Defense is no different than scouting for any other defense, and depends primarily on the proficiency of your scouts. More than enough has already been written showing the variety of forms available, etc. Like most teams, we have devised our own battery of paper work, but none of it is really unique, except, perhaps, our Offensive Tendency Summary. While this chart is something less than an IBM print-out, it does put on a single meaningful page all of the data needed to quickly ascertain D and D tendencies, hash tendencies and formation tendencies (Figure 5-1).

The progression from accumulated data to a workable game plan is, of course, a personal and flexible one, which varies from week to week and depends primarily on the capabilities and personalities of the coaches on your staff. Because of this, we do not have a formalized system established at the staff echelon, but each staff member is familiar with the "Notes for Defensive Captains" which does serve as a guideline for all of our thinking. Once established, the game plan will be communicated to our defensive captains through a thorough discussion of these notes.

NOTES FOR DEFENSIVE CAPTAINS

A. General information that *must* be known:

    1. Complete understanding of the Invert Defense.

Long before we can go about the process of establishing specific defensive game plans, the captain will have to be as well schooled in the total defensive concept as any other staff member. We have found that this is best accomplished in short informal sessions before season, where small segments of the defense are dissected, evaluated and related to the total concept.

    2. Personnel: Strengths, weaknesses and personalities.

A rapport must be established between coach and captain that will permit, with strict confidence, an exchange of ideas regarding the strengths, weaknesses and limitations of each defensive player. Just as an offensive QB is going to go to his best back over the best blocker in most critical situations, the captain must recognize which invert is better deep in passing situations, which firing linebacker is more effective on pass rush, and if one

Summarize the findings of the offensive statistic sheets on this.

	FORMATION			FORMATION			FORMATION		
	YDle	hash	play	YDle	hash	play	YDle	hash	play
1 / 10									
2 s h o r t									
2 l o n g									
3 s h o r t									
3 l o n g									

FIGURE 5-1
Offensive Tendency Chart

of the tackles is more mobile than the other. Finally, the captain must know which players thrive on praise and encouragement, and which must be pushed.

   3.   Strengths and weaknesses of each defensive call.

   Every variation of the defense has particular reasons for being included in the entire scheme. Accepting the axiom that a complete defense requires 12 players, there must be corresponding weaknesses for each call. We simply prepare a list of all potential calls, and have the captains make notes on the strengths and weaknesses of each. During the early season, we exchange ideas on the relative strengths of each call. It is important to note that we do not prepare the list on our own and simply ask the players to digest it. Instead, the players are asked to make the analysis, thus requiring them to evaluate each call. This might take a little longer but it pays dividends in the long run, for it is through these discussions that the captains begin to fully understand the potentials of the Invert Defense.

   4.   Understanding our general defensive philosophy.

   Our defensive objectives, and the factors involved in achieving them, have been summarized in a ten-part philosophy of defense. This philosophy represents our staff's thinking on how defensive success can best be achieved. It includes goals, cautions and general directions for the field captain.

B. General defensive philosophy:

   1.   Keep opponent from scoring on a long gainer. *Pursuit.*

   Many big games have been decided by the psychological edge established when the opponent's break-away was caught short of the goal line by an outstanding individual effort, and followed with a team goal-line stand. During the course of any season, a few plays are bound to break away, but these can be significantly reduced, if a total commitment has been made to *pursuit.* Later in this chapter we will discuss how we have worked to make good pursuit synonymous with River Dell Football.

   2.   Force turnover by:

    a.   Gang-tackling all of the time.
    b.   Force offensive error on 1st down
    c.   Force interception on pass down .

Forcing turnovers is probably the most reliable statistic that can be used to evaluate a quality defense. One of our weekly Defensive Goals is to force a minimum of three turnovers. We believe that field position and momentum are the keys to winning games, and each turnover roughly equals a 30-yard reversal in field position and has obvious psychological effects. Turnovers don't just happen, they are sought after. Players must talk about them, pull and grab for them and be consciously alert to take possession of "their ball." Awareness to tendencies on various D and D situations increases the opportunity to think pass, and thus insures the best combination of pressure and coverage for each passing down.

3. Create a long-yardage situation with *forcing* defenses.

When evaluating the strengths and weaknesses of each defensive call, we place each into a general category of *forcing* or *containing* calls. Basically, forcing calls are those involving some type of stunt or pre-determined commitment in the forcing unit and provide a high percentage of plays for a loss, while being more susceptible to a substantial gain if the stunt is picked up in the offensive blocking pattern. Contain calls, as is implied in their name, are designed to stretch but not break under offensive pressure, yielding perhaps three yards but consistently eliminating the big gainer.

A long-yardage situation is defined as one in which the offense must average four or more yards on each remaining down, excluding a kicking down. If you are not successful in creating the long-yardage situation on the 1–10 call, repeat it or another call from the forcing category.

4. Once long-yardage is created, use *contain* defenses to produce a kicking situation.

Our contain calls generally include those calls that will provide a maximum of pursuit with a minimum of predetermined commitment. In accordance with our philosophy on turnovers, we took a chance to cause an error on first down, and now must work to establish a definite passing situation or force our opponent to give up the ball by kicking.

5. In passing situations we prefer to *cover*, but in opposition territory, or in midfield, we will *pressure* often. *Pressure* good passers often, *cover* average passers always.

Calls in the cover category result in a four-man rush with seven men involved in zone coverage. We prefer this type of call on most passing downs because we feel that any one of the front four might individually whip his man, providing us with the desired pressure while we achieve maximum coverage. Of course, a steady diet of this type of defense can prove disastrous, especially against a fine passer. Thus on pressure calls, we'll commit five, six or seven men to pressure the passer. Rather than rushing "across the board," we prefer to limit the pass rush to one specific point of attack which has been selected on the basis of scouting. For example, if against a dropback passing attack where the strongside guard would check the LB and then help outside, a Chuckles Special Fire would be our preferred pressure call (Figure 5-2).

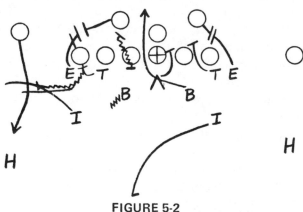

FIGURE 5-2

Chuckles Special Fire vs. Pass

6. The closer we are to our own goal line, the more willing we must become to take a chance.

The statisticians tell us that the longer the drive, the more likely an offense becomes to stop itself with an error or penalty. Conversely, the closer it is to your goal line, or the shorter the drive needed for a score, the greater the pressure on the defense. We have set up a complete goal-line defense philosophy that parallels our normal defensive thinking with regard to creating long-yardage situations by forcing the following up with calls designed to contain. I've read that a pass defender should never let a receiver behind him, but that doesn't necessarily hold up when you are defending in the end zone. Immediately tackling a receiver after a catch in the end zone is of little value; that is the time to take a chance and clearly step in front of him to deny the completion.

7. The deeper we have an opponent in his own territory, the more aggressive we can become inside and the more cautious we must be in containment and depth.

The first thing we can expect from an opponent caught deep in his own territory is that he will fight inside for running room with direct thrusts into the line. While we want to make the going in that area as tough as possible, we can not totally commit to it without weakening containment and secondary coverage. Often in this situation we will use a rush call on first and second down (diagrammed in Figure 5-3 and discussed in Chapter 8), and some type of containing call on third down.

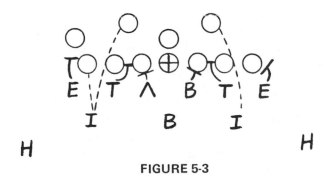

FIGURE 5-3

Rush Defense (Aggressive Force, Stable Contain)

8. We must play against *tendencies* first. You should know what defensive call works best against the opponent's best plays. If you expect a particular play, that call is the one to make.

Practicing the week of a game, we want to work only against those sets and plays that we truly anticipate our opponent will run. Much of the mental preparation for each defensive player is spent recognizing sets and keys that tell him what play affecting him might be run. Against each play in the opponent's repertoire, we should have a particular call that we prefer. When down and distance, field position and game situation dictate that play, we want to be making that call.

9. The defense has done its job if:

   a. It prevents the opponent from scoring.
   b. It gives the ball to our offense outside of our defensive pride zone—an even better job.
   c. Five times each game we want to give the ball to our offense inside the 50-yard line.
   d. Occasionally, a great defense will score a few TD's of its own. We'd like one each game.

Setting meaningful goals can sometimes be a problem. If they are not attainable often enough they lose significance, while goals achieved in defeat are tarnished, to say the least. By including the goals in a progression, we can make them as high as we want, placing special emphasis on the really great things a defense can do, without creating the feeling that we have failed if we do not get a defensive score on every series of downs.

With our coaching staff platooned, as described earlier, the Head Coach has the responsibility of getting the defense to think offensively: that is, insuring that they recognize their job doesn't end with preventing a score; it begins at that point. We go back to establishing field position and reversing momentum, the keys to victory. Probably the finest defensive unit we ever coached had the distinction of giving up nearly twice as many points as several of our other great clubs, but they had the misfortune to be coupled with an offense that lacked maturity, and with an unusually weak kicking game. One-half of the scores they gave up resulted from drives of less than ten yards. That defensive unit, however, led us to another State Championship, and they did it by causing 30 turnovers and limiting our nine opponents to 936 yards of total offense.

10. There are three defensive positions on the field:

a. Offensive Pride Zone—when we have our opponent backed inside his own 20-yard line.
b. Between the 20-yard lines.
c. Defensive Pride Zone—a 20-yard test of our pride.

With the change in ball position on the field, there is a corresponding change in the personality portrayed by a defense. In the Offensive Pride Zone, we strive for a cool confidence; their backs are to the wall, and we'll not let them escape. Our offense can and will score following the punt *we force* or mistake *they* make. Most of the game will be played between the 20's, and the winners in a close game will most likely be the opportunists, the team that forces the other into a critical error. We have to begin thinking offensively here on defense, for simply forcing a punt will not suffice; it will put our offense at a disadvantage, and following an exchange of kicks we'll probably be right back in the same place. A turnover in this zone will reverse momentum and field position. In the Defensive Pride Zone the advantage becomes ours because pride is on our side. Offenses tend to become more conservative in this zone, and our fanatical determination to be the best on defense becomes more overt. We look to our captain for leadership and strength. We recall with pride that our champions of the past have been here before and held, and resolve that we will hold also. Nothing destroys an offense more than to bring it into this zone and not be able to score. Again, our Goal-Line Defense will reverse the game's momentum. It takes *pride* in this zone.

C. Use of Scouting Information

By the time that the captain is being involved in the planning, the decisions have already been made on what adjustments will be made to compensate for various offensive strengths of the opponent. The Defensive Coach and the captain will review the following checklist to insure that the captain fully understands what areas we are particularly concerned with:

Scout Information Checklist

1. Have a basic understanding of opponent's (a) personnel, (b) style of play, and (c) formation variations.
2. What adjustments (if any) are we making to compensate for particular formations, plays, personnel, etc.? Why?

3. What are their most dangerous plays? (Our best call for each is_____ .)
4. Do they have any definite down-distance tendencies? (Our best call for each is _____.)
5. Do they have any definite hashmark tendencies? (Our best call is _____ .)
6. Are there any "special" plays that we must look for? (Under what conditions, how do we best defend them?)

THE DEFENSIVE CALL SHEET

A general Defensive Call Sheet has been set up on the basis of the general information regarding our defense and our defensive philosophy. The format (Figure 5-4) is simple and contains all the information needed to make the best defensive calls under normal circumstances. For each special week, this call sheet will be reviewed and possible calls reduced in each category, and any special calls that are to be used that week will be added.

Calls have been separated into *forcing, contain, short yardage, pressure and cover* categories, as well as into three divisions according to hashmark position. The basic category of call is selected from the Down & Distance block in the right hand corner. On 1-10, for example, we would normally call a forcing call, and use a contain call as a change of pace. If the ball were located on the defensive left hash, 1-10, we would likely call Monster Blood, or perhaps a Chuckles Thunder or Scream'n Hawk. For any given week, each category would contain only two, or at most three, possible calls. Rules covering the basic Split-End Adjustments, discussed in Chapter 1, and the Goal Line Defense calls are included here to serve as a reminder to the captain as he reviews for the game. In addition to the Call Sheet which is given every week, the notes taken during the discussion of scouting information will be summarized and attached.

We like to have the meetings with the captains completed by Tuesday, allowing Tuesday and Wednesday practices to test the plan for possible weaknesses, and then on Thursday a copy of the Call Sheet and Notes will be posted, and individual copies given to each coach and defensive captain.

It is desirable in practice to have a play sheet prepared for the scout team with copies for the Head Coach and Defensive

DEFENSIVE CALL SHEET		
LEFT	CENTER	RIGHT
FORCING CALLS	FORCING CALLS	FORCING CALLS
MONSTER BLOOD	MON/CHUC X-FIRE	CHUCKLES BLOOD
Monster X-Fire	Mon/Chuc Fire	Chuckles X-Fire
Monster Sp Fire		Chuckles SP Fire
Chuckles Thunder	Mon/Chuc Thunder	Monster Thunder
Scream'n Hawk	Scream'n Hawk	Scream'n Hawk
CONTAIN CALLS	CONTAIN CALLS	CONTAIN CALLS
MONSTER (St,A,M,Gap)	MONSTER	CHUCKLES (St,A,M,Gap)
Chuc Away/Gap	CHUCKLES	Mon Away/Gap
Monster Blood		Chuckles Blood
Hawk Level Right		Hawk Level Left
SHORT YARDAGE	SHORT YARDAGE	SHORT YARDAGE
Rush	RUSH	Rush
MON BLOOD-X-Fire	Mon/Chuc Blood-X-Fire	CHUC BLOOD-X-FIRE
PRESSURE CALLS	PRESSURE CALLS	PRESSURE CALLS
Monster X-Fire	Chuckles X-Fire	Chuckles X-Fire
Chuckles Sp Fire	Mon Sp Fire	Monster Sp Fire
Scream'n Hawk	Scream'n Hawk	Scream'n Hawk
COVER CALLS	COVER CALLS	COVER CALLS
CHUCKLES AWAY	MONSTER	MONSTER AWAY
Monster Blood	Chuckles	Chuckles Blood
Hawk Level Right	Hawk Level Rt/Lt	Hawk Level Lt
HAWK LOCK-ON	HAWK LOCK-ON	HAWK LOCK-ON

SPLIT-END ADJUSTMENTS	DOWN & DISTANCE CALLS
NORMAL — SE to *wide side,* anticipate wide side play or action pass to SE.	1-10: FORCE/contain
	2-6 (or less): FORCE
EAGLE — SE to *short side,* anticipate inside or strong side play or pass.	2-6 to 10: CONTAIN
COVER — Definite PASS situation.	2-10 (or more): PASS (pressure/cover)
GOAL LINE AND SHORT YARDAGE DEFENSE	3-4 (or less): FORCE
RUSH — used in mid-field short yardage down or when offense must average 4 or more yards in goal line situation.	3-4 to 7: CONTAIN
	3-7 (or more): PASS (cover/pressure)

GOAL LINE MONSTER/CHUCKLES — Normal goal
line defense, opponent must avg.
2-4 yds. on each remaining play.
GOAL LINE PRIDE — Total commitment defense,
we MUST stop them for NO GAIN.

FIGURE 5-4

Defensive Call Sheet

Coordinator. Thus every call will be meaningful to each player and we can get every defensive player thinking in terms of specific tendencies.

SAMPLE DEFENSIVE GAME PLAN

On the basis of all available scouting information, final plans are made, discussed with the captains and posted. The Offensive Tendency Chart is also duplicated so that each player has the opportunity to review those plays and sets that affect him the most. While all available information is retained in an active file, the Tendency Chart, Call Sheet and Scouting Notes Summary are kept readily available. In this particular sample, we have only 40 plays charted on the Tendency Chart (Figure 5-5), while we might normally expect to have double that number if we have scouted them twice and have charted the previous year's film.

The Scouting Summary, Figure 5-6, contains the answers to questions raised in the Scouting Checklist, as well as declarations of all keys and reminders of important Coaching Points. It serves as a "Ready List" for all defensive players.

The revised Defensive Call Sheet, Figure 5-7, is the concern of the captain and Defensive Coordinator only. The captain is expected to make all of his calls on the field within the framework of this sheet. One standard exception—when, as the game progresses, a pattern of predictable calls develops for the offense, the call best suited to stop a particular play should be substituted.

Sometimes, factors other than the scouting report will dictate additions or deletions from the call sheet. In this game, for example, all Hawk Defenses have been eliminated because it was felt that they weren't needed, and extensive use of the Hawk was planned for the following week.

RELENTLESS PURSUIT IS A STATE OF MIND

The common denominator that brings together the individual skills and personalities that make up the forcing unit is team pursuit. The willingness of our athletes to subject themselves to the pain and pressure of relentless pursuit is developed in a positive manner and is fostered by individual pride. Awareness of

Summarize the findings of the offensive statistic sheets on this chart.

	FORMATION			FORMATION			FORMATION		
	YDLE	HASH	PLAY	YDLE	HASH	PLAY	YDLE	HASH	PLAY
1/10	−20	M	47 DIVE(RT.)	−25	R	BLAST LT.	−40	M	37 BELLY (RT.)
	−32	L	49 JET(RT.)	−36	M	37 BELLY(RT.)	+47	R	19 ROLL(RT.)
	−25	M	34 DIVE(LT.)	+25	L	37 BELLY (RT.)	+49	L	49 BELLY PITCH (RT.)
	−40	M	41 SWEEP(LT.)	−28	M	TB POWER(RT.)	−35	R	11 ROLL (LT.)
	+35	R	41 SWEEP(LT.)						
	−38	M	42 SLANT						
2 SHORT				−47	L	BLAST LT.	−47	R	TB POWER RT.
				+28	L	BLAST LT.			
				−35	M	BLAST LT.			
2 LONG	−30	M	27 CTR. TRAP	−22	R	BLAST LT.	−28	M	49 BELLY PITCH(RT.)
	+45	R	42 SLANT	−27	R	BLAST LT.	+49	M	ROLL LT. PASS
	+24	M	42 SLANT	−38	M	49 BELLY PITCH	−34	L	ORBIT 29 SWEEP (RT.)
	−41	L	27 CTR. TRAP						
3 SHORT	−28	L	BLAST LT.	−33	R	BLAST LT.			
				+26	L	FB WEDGE			
				−37	M	FB WEDGE			
3 LONG	+45	R	ROLL LT. SCREEN RT.				−32	R	ROLL LT. PASS
	+49	L	CB PASS IN B MIDDLE SCREEN				−30	M	ROLL LT. PASS
							−40	R	ROLL LT. PASS
							+22	M	49 BELLY PITCH
							−32	M	ROLL LT. PASS
							−43	M	ROLL LT. PASS

FIGURE 5-5

Offensive Tendency Chart

SCOUT INFORMATION SUMMARY

Multiple-T formation led by outstanding run/pass QB, #10, Murray. They show definite formation tendencies, and a stronger than normal tendency to run to the wide side.

Wing-T	Power-I	Slot-I
Sweep	Blast to	Roll Pass to
Dive/slant	Belly away	Belly away
Ctr trap	Wedge away	TB power away
Jet		

POWER-I ADJUSTMENTS: If Power is *toward* you—

DE—automatic Blood, across face if loop is away, across butt if our loop is to you.

LB, T & M—If our loop is to the power, automatic *Mike*; if loop is opposite from power, automatic *away*. First step with outside leg, penetrate.

PASSING SITUATIONS: Call Chuckles Crossfire, anticipating Slot-I formation. Roll Lt Pass. If another set, cancel Crossfire, look for screen, option or reverse.

BEST PLAYS: Blast Left—   Power-I Adjustments
                Roll Left Pass— Chuckles Crossfire
                I-Belly Option— Chuckles Blood, Mon Crossfire

D & D TENDENCIES:

| 3-long-Slot-I | Roll Pass— | Chuc Crossfire |
| 2/3-short | PIR Blast— | PIR Adjustments |

HASHMARK TENDENCIES: Stronger than average tendency to wide side.

SPECIAL PLAYS: Shotgun pass formation—automatic 4-3 Lock-on

KEYS: Inverts key the *Middle Back,* switch on motion
          Linebackers key—*Normal,* near setback/QB

COACHING POINTS:

Be conscious of #17 at TB; he is former QB and will throw Sweep Pass. If QB rolls to our *Loop Tackle,* tackle should support contains, Invert will be covering flat.

Be prepared to make *hammer* adjustment in game if we have trouble with the split-end on sweep from Slot formation.

FIGURE 5-6

Scout Summary

DEFENSIVE CALL SHEET

LEFT	CENTER	RIGHT
FORCING CALLS	FORCING CALLS	FORCING CALLS
MONSTER BLOOD	MON/CHUC X-FIRE	CHUCKLES BLOOD
Monster X-Fire	Mon/Chuc Fire	Chuckles X-Fire
~~Monster Sp Fire~~		~~Chuckles Sp Fire~~
Chuckles Thunder	~~Mon/Chuc Thunder~~	Monster Thunder
~~Scream'n Hawk~~	~~Scream'n Hawk~~	~~Scream'n Hawk~~
CONTAIN CALLS	CONTAIN CALLS	CONTAIN CALLS
MONSTER (St,A,M,Gap)	MONSTER	CHUCKLES (St,A,M,Gap)
Chuc Away/Gap	CHUCKLES	Mon Away/Gap
Monster Blood		Chuckles Blood
~~Hawk Level Right~~		~~Hawk Level Left~~
SHORT YARDAGE	SHORT YARDAGE	SHORT YARDAGE
~~Rush~~	RUSH	Rush
MON BLOOD-X-Fire	Mon/~~Chuc~~-Blood-X-Fire	~~CHUC BLOOD-X-FIRE~~
PRESSURE CALLS	PRESSURE CALLS	PRESSURE CALLS
~~Monster X-Fire~~	Chuckles X-Fire	Chuckles X-Fire
Chuckles Sp Fire	~~Mon Sp Fire~~	~~Monster Sp Fire~~
~~Scream'n Hawk~~	~~Scream'n Hawk~~	~~Scream'n Hawk~~
COVER CALLS	COVER CALLS	COVER CALLS
CHUCKLES AWAY	MONSTER	MONSTER AWAY
Monster Blood	Chuckles	Chuckles Blood
~~Hawk Level Right~~	~~Hawk Level Rt/Lt~~	~~Hawk Level Lt~~
~~HAWK LOCK ON~~	~~HAWK LOCK ON~~	~~HAWK LOCK ON~~

SPLIT-END ADJUSTMENTS

NORMAL — SE to *wide side*, anticipate wide side play or action pass to SE.

EAGLE — SE to *short side*, anticipate inside or strong side play or pass.

~~COVER — Definite PASS situation.~~

GOAL LINE AND
SHORT YARDAGE DEFENSE

RUSH — used in mid-field short yardage down or when offense must average 4 or more yards in goal line situation.

GOAL LINE MONSTER/CHUCKLES — Normal goal line defense, opponent must avg. 2-4 yds. on each remaining play.

GOAL LINE PRIDE — Total commitment defense, we MUST stop them for NO GAIN.

DOWN & DISTANCE CALLS

1-10: FORCE/contain

2-6 (or less): FORCE

2-6 to 10: CONTAIN

2-10 (or more): PASS
(pressure/cover)

3-4 (or less): FORCE

3-4 to 7: CONTAIN

3-7 (or more): PASS
(cover/pressure)

FIGURE 5-7

Revised Call Sheet, Sample Game Plan

each player's movement on every play in practice requires the concentration of several coaches. Praise and reward are heaped on any player who is aggressive moving to the football, who has been blocked and fights to recover, and particularly one who has been cut down and instantly recovers his balance and pursuit angle. As attention of the coaches is directed to pursuit, the players are quick to pick up this emphasis, and in no time at all are pressuring themselves and their teammates to get to the ball.

While attitude is obviously the most important facet in developing pursuit, agility and understanding of pursuit angles also play an important role. Agility and body control during pursuit are developed in the normal Agility Period and in the Pursuit Sled Drills that are included in every daily practice. Acquiring a feel for the proper angle of pursuit is the result of concentration on that aspect of the game in daily teamwork drills and in our weekly Pursuit Springs.

Agility Drills cover a broad spectrum of activities, but we are most interested in those requiring movement from an up-to-down and back-up-again position. An emphasis is placed upon quick feet and immediate response to visual stimuli.

PURSUIT SLED DRILLS

SLIDE (Figure 5-8)

Coaching Points: Deliver a solid blow at each pad, stepping with same leg. Don't cross feet as you shuffle, keep butt low and head up. Rapid foot action.

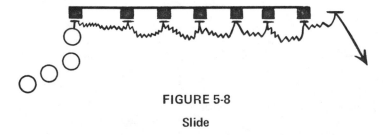

FIGURE 5-8

Slide

UPRIGHT SPINNING (Figure 5-9)

Coaching Points: Don't raise up after delivering blow, push off the pad while swinging trail arm to increase rotational speed. Slide to every other pad delivering blow with lead arm.

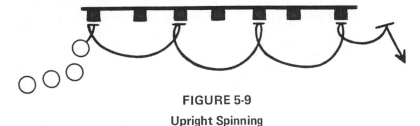

FIGURE 5-9

Upright Spinning

BUTT ROLLS

Coaching Points: Same alternate pad movement as above, but keep facing forward, rolling over on butt after extending into sled. Scramble to next pad and explode again from four-point position.

PURSUIT SPRINTS (Figure 5-10)

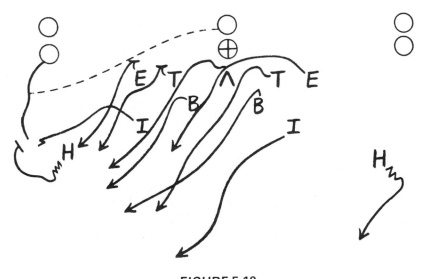

FIGURE 5-10

Pursuit Sprints

Coaching Points: A defensive sprint builder, we like to end practice with this sprint at least once weekly. The defensive unit lines up and pursues the football which can be thrown out to a wide receiver to either side of the formation. *Every* defender must touch the ballcarrier before the drill ends.

GRADE "A" FOR THE FORCING UNIT

The letter "A" symbolizes excellence to essentially all of us who work in athletics and education. We believe that the forcing unit on the Invert Defense has a framework built on *A*ctivity, *A*gility and *A*ttitude. Successful application of the techniques and principles outlined in these first five chapters depends upon the enthusiasm and understanding shown by the coaching staff. They have been successful at River Dell because we believe in them, and we have seen them succeed in other schools for the same reasons.

6

Coaching the Invert
Defensive Secondary

In the long run, success on defense can be evaluated in terms of the success of the defensive secondary. We are very proud of what our secondary unit has been able to establish as standards of excellence at River Dell High School.

WHY INVERT THE SECONDARY

They say that "beauty is in the eye of the beholder," and nothing could be more applicable in explaining why we feel that the Invert Defense is at home in high school football. Like most innovations in the game today, the Invert concept was born and bred of necessity at the major college level for reasons not necessarily valid in high school. It was in college that coaches deeply rooted in zone pass defensive philosophy had to contend with offensive formations that spread their cornerbacks so wide that they could not effectively establish a short corner against the sweep. Just who was the first to exchange the cornerback and inside safety's responsibility could probably be debated at length, but the important thing is that it occurred, and coupled with it was the opportunity to disguise your pass coverage from Invert zone to man and combination. While these were problems of significance to major college coaches, they were of little consequence to the high school mentor who still saw two tight ends and a wingback in nine out of ten games. Thus we did not see the Invert Defense permeate the high school circles until much later and for very different reasons.

As discussed in Chapter 1, initially it was our desire to simultaneously defend the corner and deep pass more effectively that led us to inverting the secondary. The overall effect on the forcing unit has been explained, but the area that benefited most from the change was, of course, the defensive secondary.

The inverted alignment seemed to challenge our opponents to throw more often than we had ever experienced, and far in excess of tendencies exhibited against other teams. With the increase in passing, our opposition experienced a decrease in their ability to control the football, thus having a positive effect on our overall defense. In a recent year the opposition attempted 156 passes in our nine games, completing 50, while we intercepted 27, better than one interception for every two completed.

Two factors appear to have accounted for our ability to maintain such an effective level of pass defense in an alignment that presents its strength against the run: the placement of our best pass defenders in the deep outside zones, where they are relieved from initial run responsibilities, and the encouragement to develop defensive specialists in the secondary, who can spend all of their practice time refining the skills that are pertinent to their responsibilities.

The potential to cover two wide-outs and disguise our pass coverage still exists within the Invert secondary, but unlike our college counterparts, we find that it is unnecessary to change up in our coverages very often, and not at all with our younger players. The simplicity, instead, accounts for the success we have had.

The temptation to throw the bomb, a low-percentage play to start with, against our invert, who appears to be crowding the line of scrimmage before the snap but always seems to be back in the nick of time, has broken the continuity of many otherwise sound offensive drives.

SELECTING PERSONNEL

Too often, to the dismay of college recruiters, the top high school athletes are limited in size and don't have truly great speed to compensate for it. When we first considered using the Invert Defense, we questioned whether we had the kind of personnel required. We found an abundant supply, because at Invert we needed a boy who was quick, aggressive and agile. He did not need great speed or size. We found by chance that wrestlers often filled the bill better than anyone. Over the years we have had some outstanding inverts, usually about 5'8" and 135 pounds, including two regional wrestling champions and several others who exhibited similar physical qualities. The inverts are the hub of our defense, and it is no coincidence that the outstanding characteristic of most of them has been their intense personal pride. Pride accounts for their presence in the "big man's game," and their contagious spirit is part of what makes our defense what it is.

The contrast in appearance and personality between our inverts and halfbacks is startling. While the invert is small and aggressive, often high strung, the halfbacks tend to be the opposite. We generally look to basketball players to man the halfback positions. We like a halfback to be about six feet tall, with good speed, hands and jumping ability. His basic responsibility is to play pass defense against the best receivers that our opponent can offer. We'd like him to be cool-headed and slightly conservative. If he happens to be a hitter, and we have had a few, then that is a bonus, but all we require with regard to being a tackler is that he prevent the ballcarrier from getting past, and that he can avoid being knocked down by an open-field blocker. Because the position is so easy to learn and depends to such a great extent on the innate ability of the player, we have found that these players often can serve as back-up receivers for our offensive unit or as specialists in the kicking game.

As previously indicated, we try to encourage the development of defensive specialists in the secondary. As you can see by reviewing the selection criteria, we are not looking for superior athletes, the ones who will be the top QB or favored running back; instead, we seek boys who probably wouldn't make the first eleven on an eleven-man squad. Consequently, as early as the freshman year, we begin to platoon our football players. The inverts, in particular, will probably never play an offensive play in four years of high school football. Because of the success we have enjoyed and the pride that has been developed, this is no problem at all. It would not be unusual to come across a "little rascal" in our seventh grade whose ambition in life is to become an invert at River Dell High School.

THE PYRAMID OF PASS DEFENSE

Scanning a few coaching journals or browsing through any coach's book shelf will provide a source of many defensive alignments, all basically sound, and most likely followed with a list of drills used to incorporate the defensive scheme. We are all well aware of the fact that there is more to it than that. Several years ago we were fortunate enough to be able to spend some time with Lee Royer, formerly coach of the secondary at the U.S. Naval Academy. We talked about establishing a learning progression for defensive backs, a method of incorporating the learned individual skills into a unified philosophy of team pass defense. We incorporated his ideas, which were 3-deep-zone oriented, into our own invert philosophy, and from it has evolved what we feel is the most compact and complete coaching guide available for defensive backs. We expect every boy who is going to play in our secondary to understand thoroughly the Pyramid of Pass Defense (Figure 6-1).

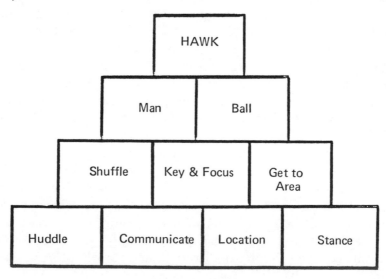

FIGURE 6-1

The Pyramid of Pass Defense

HUDDLE. Don't turn your back on the offense. Know the down, distance, field position and tendencies of the offense. *Be sure of the defensive call.* Look for someone leaving the offensive huddle.

For a defensive back, the next play begins as the previous play is ending. He should *be alert* to calls or signals from the opponent's bench. As he enters the defensive huddle, having already noted the down, distance and field position, he should be asking himself, "What did our scouting report indicate as a tendency for this situation?"

COMMUNICATE. After the huddle breaks, *communicate* with the other defensive backs regarding individual responsibilities and opposition tendencies.

Two coaching points are important here: (1) there should be a single leader or captain of this unit, one boy who is capable and interested in doing the little extra in the way of game preparation, and (2) as the opponent's offensive huddle breaks, a general pattern of conversation should unfold regarding the declaration of keys, formation tendencies and the recognition of receiving threats. Assuming that an offense is aligned in a Pro-set with a flanker to the wide side on a secondary and long situation, a typical commentary might go like this:

LHB (captain) calls "Pro-left, Pro-left," then to the Left Invert declares, "Check the crackback." In turn, the Left Invert calls the inverts' key to the RI, "35, 35." The RI, anticipating that he will be going back to the deep-middle, reminds the RHB that he will need help defending the SE on a post route, "Help on the post, close down our seam."

This type of communication is basic to sound defensive play in the secondary.

LOCATION. *Halfbacks:* Basic alignment is 4 yards wider than a tight end and 7 yards deep (Figure 6-2).
Note: Always be at least 1 yard wider than the widest receiver until you reach a point where you can "cover him to the boundary" (Figure 6-3). For example, if the ball was on one hash, you could probably move inside a split-receiver at the other hash and still cover him to the sideline. However, if the ball were at mid-field, you would still remain on his outside until he split closer to the sideline.

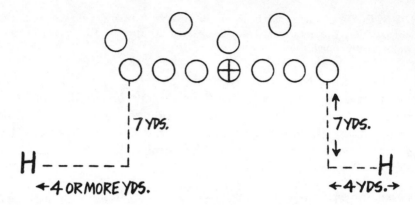

FIGURE 6-2

Halfback Location

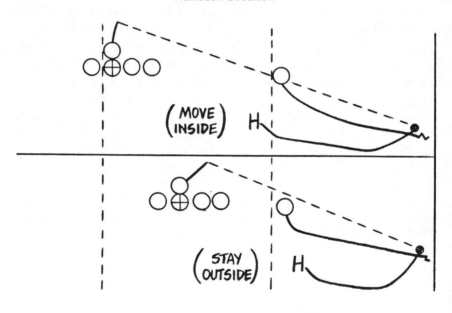

FIGURE 6-3

"Cover to Boundary" Point Varies with Ball Position

LOCATION. *Inverts:* Invert alignment is always along opposite sides of the Invert Triangle. Normal positions for both inverts is to be in the T-E gap, a full 3 yards deep. Pre-inverting moves one invert toward the *up* position and the other *deep*, still maintaining their opposite relationship with each other. (Figure 6-4 shows the Invert Triangle.)

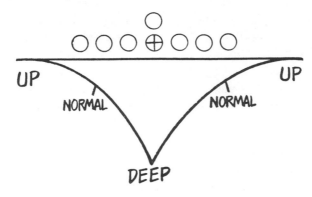

FIGURE 6-4

The Invert Triangle

The Invert Triangle is probably the most distinguishing feature of our Invert Defense philosophy. In most descriptions we have seen, the four backs of the secondary line up "across the board," and on flow to his side, the inside safety moves *laterally* until forward movement of the ball is established, then he fills off-tackle. This, in effect, neutralizes most of the strengths previously attributed to the invert secondary in our earlier discussion. In particular, it forces the invert to take on the power sweep "face to face," and precludes the use of the wrestler-type invert. Instead, we require that initial movement be along the line of the triangle. On movement of the key, the one invert will be retreating along the triangle to the *deep* position, while the other shuffles to the *up* position from where he will establish his defense of the corner or shuffle back into the flat. As we'll explain further into our discussion of the Pass Pyramid, the invert's stance, keys and movement facilitate his play along the Triangle.

Movement along the path defined by the Triangle is not natural and must be learned. To help establish that pattern, we have the triangle lines actually drawn on our practice field in the area in which our defensive backs do their fundamental work. By drilling daily in the presence of this reminder, movement along the path becomes a conditioned reflex. Many of our game situation drills are done in this area so that the Triangle can become associated with opponent formations.

STANCE. *HBs:* Assume a breakdown position with the inside foot up, looking over the inside shoulder toward the QB. Arms should be loose and the hands free.

Inverts: Assume a breakdown position, but feet must be parallel to the Invert Triangle. Therefore, if you are "normal," the outside foot will be forward, but in a "pre-inverted" position you would be square to the line of scrimmage.

Have you sometimes wondered what to do with that injured player who is standing around taking up space? Make him the Stance Coach. Having a good stance is critical to getting a good start, yet many of us talk about it in the beginning of the year but don't discipline it on the field. Nothing is more inviting to a scout than to see a defensive back "anchored" to the ground with his hands on his knees, or with his hands on his hips and knees straight. Having someone on the field making players constantly aware of having a correct stance is a luxury that all of us can afford.

These four items, Huddle, Communication, Location and Stance, are the base of the Pyramid. As you can see, they are learned traits, and any athlete is capable of doing them with just a little practice and understanding. Yet in the heat of a game, it is usually one of them that gives way, and like any structure with a weakened foundation, sound pass defense goes with it.

The second level of the Pyramid is based on movement, and a coordinated effort must be made on and off the field to develop an understanding by each member of the secondary of what the other is doing.

SHUFFLE. (Applies to halfbacks only.) On the snap, shuffle back and out. It is important to start your movement by taking the first step with the back (outside) foot. That keeps your weight down and allows you to *keep your shoulders over your toes*. Take three shuffles. You will probably be able to make your "read" at two, but continue with the third so that you will be under control and ready to "start all together" as you move to your area.

We have experimented with starting the shuffle movement with a crossover step because we felt that it might prove a quicker and more balanced movement. We found, however, that it tended to encourage rising up or leaning back as the player moved into his backpedal. While he might move straight backward in this raised position, it would take him several steps to "gather-up" in order to react to the ball. It is imperative that a player's shoulders be over his toes while he is moving on a football field if he intends to do anything when he arrives where he is running. Of even greater significance is guarding against the temptation of the halfback to stand flatfooted at the snap of the ball. His location has been predicated on the position of the wide receiver. If he is to stand motionless while he "reads," the receiver's position will have changed relative to his and most likely the change will be to his disadvantage. We call it "star-gazing," and it is equally dangerous for halfbacks and inverts.

KEY & FOCUS. Instead of shuffling like the halfbacks, inverts must react to the movement of a key at the snap of the ball. The purpose of the key is to direct the UP and DEEP reaction of each. *Both inverts must always key the same man.* As the *up* invert begins to move along the triangle, he reads the wide receiver for *crackback* or *push*, and levels off against the push or fights the crackback block. The time involved in moving to this new position is roughly equal to the time the HB spent shuffling. Now, all defensive backs are ready to key the QB while they focus on their receiving threats. This requires peripheral vision, a trait common to all of us, but one that must be practiced to be developed. Know where the receiver is, "sense his presence," but be looking to the QB's eyes.

Getting to the deep middle after reading a key on the snap of the ball is something that has concerned many coaches who have questioned us about the Invert Defense. In reality, it is the easier of the two reactions to make. Receivers going to the deep middle must either fight their way through the maze in front or come a longer distance. In addition, because the key is usually set to one side of the formation or the other, the inverts are able to say before the snap, "I'm going *deep* unless . . ." and "I'm coming *up* unless. . . ."

The *up* invert, on the other hand, must discipline himself to look to the wide receiver for his secondary key. It is a great temptation to follow your initial key as he fakes into the line or sets up to block the end on sprint-out pass action. Reacting to this secondary key by leveling off in the flat or avoiding the crackback block is accomplished quite easily, as we drill it regularly in practice.

The Key and Focus technique described for all defensive backs in an integral part of all zone coverage philosophies. The QB is the man controlling the football, and more often than not he will show you what he intends to do with a pass long before it is thrown.

GET TO YOUR AREA. As receivers release into your zone, begin to backpedal, and finally *skate* with the deepest one. As a halfback, maintain the outside position on him until you are confident that you can cover him to the boundary of your zone. It is not a man-to-man responsibility so you should not drift too far to either side of your zone, but if the deepest man in your zone is to the outside, defend him best. Start fast and then throttle down. Be aware of a lead receiver cutting short or across your zone, and the follow-up receiver breaking deep. Keep in mind the concept of *flexible zones*, and the extent of *your* responsibility.

Getting to your area for the three deep backs actually begins at the end of the shuffle for the halfbacks and the instant the *deep* invert has begun reacting to his key. Assuming that the ball was in the center of the field and the QB dropped straight back, this would be a very simple process, with each back assuming responsibility for slightly more than one-third of the width of the field and expecting help from undercoverage on any ball thrown less than 11 yards beyond the line of scrimmage. The only back having pressure on him would be the invert dropping to the middle. As he made his drop, he would be particularly concerned if he were backing away from two quick receivers. He can not afford to turn his back on the receiver potentially running the seam behind him as he retreats to the deep middle. However, if he reacts quickly he can square-up in the center of his zone, and then skate facing the major receiving threats.

"Skating" is the term we use to describe the technique of running with an opponent once you have been forced out of the backpedal. It is the running style that is typically incorporated in wave drills where we ask players to roll their hips as they run backwards.

Coverage of the straight dropback pass in the center of the field would look like Figure 6-5.

Movement of the ball from the center of the field, as well as from the center of the formation, puts added pressure on one particular zone or area. Thus, we instill in our players the concept of flexible zones. A quarterback sprinting or rolling out to one side of the formation is obviously more capable of passing accurately to that side, and it does not seem reasonable to ask the

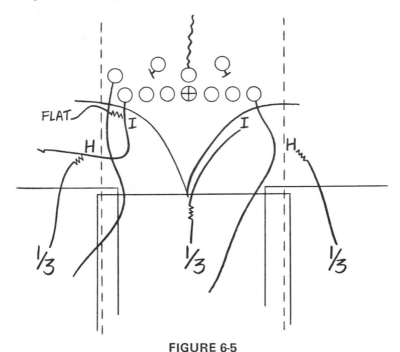

FIGURE 6-5

Basic Dropback Pass Zones

halfback to that side to defend an area as large as that defended by the halfback on the back side. We ask that our backs have sufficient speed to travel one-third the distance of the ball during flight time. The deep invert keeps the QB in the center of his zone until he begins moving toward the sideline, and then keeps the midpoint of his zone about two yards behind the QB. Since their relationship has not changed, we need not reduce the width of his zone responsibility. However, the halfback away from the QB is now further from the ball and thus should be able to defend a larger segment of the field. Since the center of the middle zone has moved toward the halfback being attacked, his zone can be narrowed, as an overlap of only two yards suffices for good zone coverage. Figure 6-6 shows what happens to the zones as the ball attacks the corner.

As the ball reverses itself on bootleg action, similar adjustments are made in the respective areas of each zone. Figure 6-7 represents the effect of bootleg action on the flexible zones.

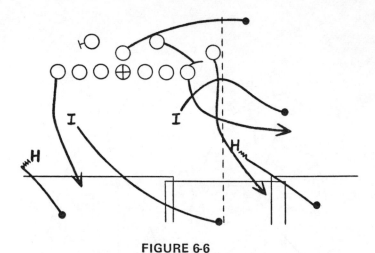

FIGURE 6-6

Flexible Zones, Ball Moving to Sideline

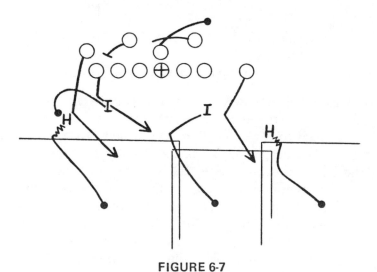

FIGURE 6-7

Flexible Zones vs. Bootleg Action

Thus far we have discussed 70 percent (7 of 10) of the steps involved in playing good pass defense. You will notice that we have placed only one physical limitation—being able to travel one-third the distance of the ball during its ball flight time—on personnel needed to play the positions. We try to sell our players on this idea. Seventy percent of success depends on how much you want to succeed, how well you understand your responsibilities, and how hard you work to have *zero defects* in the mechanics of your position.

For the remaining 30 percent of the PYRAMID, we leave the blackboard and go to the field. We stop talking and start playing. In the end, success depends upon the quality of the athletes playing the game. We have a few basic principles that apply, but in reality, once the ball is put in the air, the rules say it is free.

MAN-BALL-HAWK. On release of the ball from the quarterback, everyone is to move to the intended receiver, playing the ball *through the man*. The worst thing that a defensive back can do is to do his job properly to the point where he gets over-anxious, steps up in front and "just misses" the interception, only to see the receiver score unmolested. Play the ball *through* the man until you are *sure* of the ball, then go after it at its highest point, looking the ball into your hands. If you can't *surely* catch it clean, *search* the receiver by tearing down his arms on contact with the ball.

We tell our athletes that they have done their job properly if they are in position to immediately tackle the receiver of a completed pass. In effect, we are conceding that the opposition has come to play, and that it has on its squad some talented athletes. If, however, we can be close enough to immediately tackle the receiver, more often than not we will be close enough to play through to the ball, and either prevent the catch by "searching" the receiver, get through to knock it down, or, if it isn't thrown perfectly, move into the ball and get the Hawk (interception).

Defenders moving from other zones are approaching at an angle that will permit them to block the intended receiver if the Hawk is successful, or get a piece of the tackle if it is not. In addition, they are all aware of the "tip" potential, and they are concentrating on the ball, looking for their chance at the Hawk.

AXIOMS OF SOUND PASS DEFENSE

The mental and emotional demands of playing in the secondary far exceed the physical requirements, because every mistake is magnified and the penalty for a mistake is obvious and severe. *Confidence* is the single most important trait of each defensive back. Better understanding of the demands and limitations of their play helps build this confidence. We communicate our philosophy of pass defense to them through the following axioms:

1.   The odds are in your favor, again.

Whatever the reason might have been for an unsuccessful play, if it was stopped short of the goal the advantage goes back to the defense on the next play. On *this* play the advantage is yours. Winners take advantage of the opportunities.

2.   They'll catch the perfect pass, we'll catch the rest.

There is no adequate defense against the perfectly executed pass play except to tackle it hard immediately. With good location and movement on the ball, the defender has an equal chance at the majority of passes.

3.   Tackle the *sideline* cut and defend the *up*, or defend the *sideline* and get help on the *up*.

One man can not adequately defend both of these cuts. If you have undercoverage help, tackle the sideline, play the *up*. If you are leveling off, and have help *deep*, you can afford to play the sideline cut more aggressively.

4.   Keep on the play until the whistle has blown; nothing is worse than being beaten on a broken play.

5.   Every play is a pass until proven otherwise.

6.   The closer the ball gets to the goal line, the closer you must cover potential receivers.

Quarterbacks tend to show their intention sooner and receivers are limited in area for running their pattern. Cautious defenders tackle touchdowns in the end zone.

7.   When you get a Hawk, start directly upfield, then work toward the closest sideline.

The majority of potential tacklers are in center of field or running patterns. The straight breakaway neutralizes the other receivers, and the near sideline normally provides the safest route.

These axioms, as well as the principles previously discussed in the Pyramid, can be communicated informally in game situation discussions with the Defensive Coach.

STUNTING WITH THE INVERT SECONDARY

In the secondary, we limit stunting or change-ups to those necessary to compensate for proven offensive strengths and those needed to adequately defend the field under specific conditions. These include the addition of a fifth defensive back (to be discussed in Chapter 7), adjustments necessary to play goal-line and short-yardage defense (to be discussed in Chapter 8), and variations of our normal alignment described here.

VARYING THE INVERT KEYS

Our basic Invert key, which determines the movement along the Invert Triangle, is the "back away from the loop"—that is, the offensive back, excluding a wide flanker, to the side of the formation opposite the loop direction of the defensive line. The reasoning for this selection is that on straight dropback passes both flats will be covered, regardless of the defense called (Figure 6-8a and b).

Through scouting and sound game planning, it is our desire to determine a key that will do more than simply put us in a safe or balanced zone defense. If we can establish a key that will enable us to get an extra man at the point of attack for most of their plays, we will utilize that key until they have proven to us that they *will* take advantage of the uncovered flat. If they can find it, that is (Figure 6-9).

Adjustment of keys is a responsibility left to the coaching staff. The coach working the phones "upstairs" must be well versed in the effect of various maneuvers on our keys, so that he can distinguish between an error by one of our inverts and a play by the opponent that is creating a problem for us.

PRE-INVERTING

There often occur situations in which we would like to place a "monster" on the line to the formation strength or to the width of the field. We simply accomplish this by asking our inverts to pre-invert. By this we mean that they will move to predetermined positions along the Invert Triangle. This can be accomplished with a call to "loop away" establishing the traditional Arkansas Monster alignment, or a stunt can be used on the backside to insure defensive strength along the line of scrimmage (Figure 6-10).

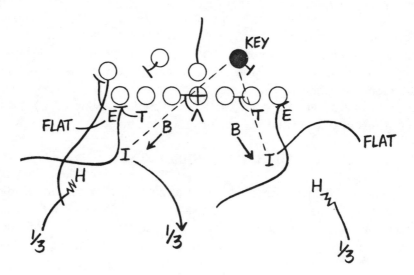

FIGURE 6-8a

Chuckles vs. Dropback Pass

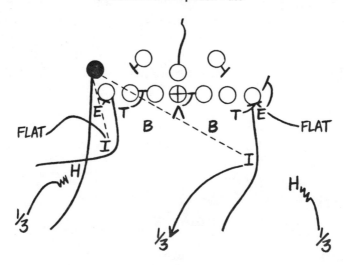

FIGURE 6-8b

Monster vs. Dropback Pass

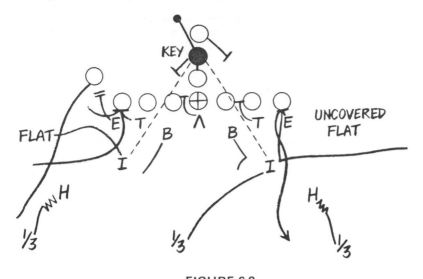

FIGURE 6-9

Chuckles, Invert Key: Fullback

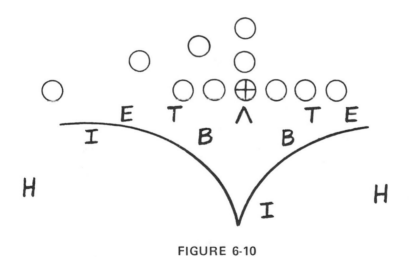

FIGURE 6-10

Pre-Inverted Alignment

If our opponent uses motion to re-establish his formation strength, we can *revert*; that is, we can move both inverts back along the Invert Triangle on the snap of the ball (Figure 6-11). If we have planned to use a lot of pre-inverting in our game plan, we might consider using 3/4 rotation against offensive action opposite

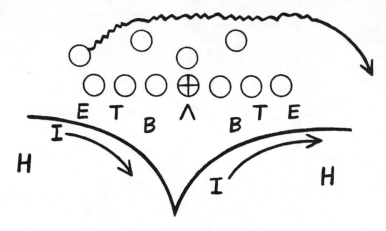

FIGURE 6-11
Inverts, Reverting on Motion

the position of our *up* invert (monster). Figure 6-12 shows the use of 3/4 rotation to compensate for play action opposite the pre-inverted set.

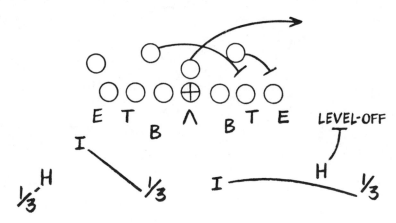

FIGURE 6-12
3/4 Rotation on Flow from Pre-Invert

LOCK-ON COVERAGE

Usually reserved for use with our fifth defensive back in the line-up, we can "lock on" in man-to-man coverage with a free safety from our normal alignment. In Figure 6-13 we combine the lock-on coverage with a double-fire.

FREE SAFETY-I

FIGURE 6-13

Chuckles-Double Fire with Lock-on Coverage

THUNDER

A "fun" call, the Thunder is nothing more than a Safety-Blitz. Combined with a linebacker fire to the inside, it has proven very successful as a first down call, designed to create the long-yardage situation. Invert action is predetermined, the *deep* invert going to the deep-middle, regardless of play action. The tackle and end on the side of the thunderer loop out to create a "seam" as the invert fires in the guard-tackle gap. His responsibility: "Make something happen." (See Figure 6-14.)

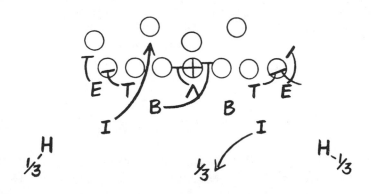

FIGURE 6-14

Monster Special Fire, Thunder

HAMMER

An invert's greatest vulnerability is to the crackback block of a man split four to seven yards from the formation. We teach our defenders that a flanker can take one of three positions (Figure 6-15) along the line, and must be checked regularly.

FIGURE 6-15

Flanker Positions

A tight wing (#1) will have a difficult block trying to hook our invert, and the halfback is in ideal position to give corner support as soon as the wing commits himself to blocking the invert. If the flanker lines up excessively wide (#3), isolating the HB, we feel he is too far removed from the play to be an effective crackback blocker without risking a clipping penalty. A split of 4-7 yards (#2), we consider to be most dangerous. From that angle, the flanker has the advantage over the invert and the halfback must respect the flanker's delayed route. If the offense proves that they will hurt us from that set, we will change off with the Hammer calls. On the Hammer, if the invert's key comes toward him he will retreat to the deep-outside, while the halfback levels off, assuming corner and flat responsibility. If the invert's key went away, it would have no effect on their play. Figure 6-16 shows how the Hammer neutralizes the crackback block of the close flanker.

DEVELOPING SKILLS THROUGH DRILLS

As indicated earlier in this text, our defensive coach is specifically responsible for coaching the defensive backs. He will normally have them for 32 minutes before being joined by the offensive coach for up to 15 minutes of skeleton drills. The first eight minutes of the 32 are devoted to the type of agility and

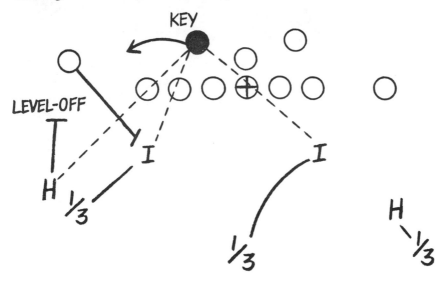

FIGURE 6-16

The Hammer Adjustment

reaction drills that are basic to essentially every football program (and that will not be discussed in this book). Of the remaining 24 minutes, it is expected that the coach will cover one of the tackling drills for approximately four minutes, and during the final 20 minutes will cover some variety of the individual and paired drills that we incorporate into our defensive secondary planning. To facilitate his planning, and to insure that each of the drills is covered, the schedule shown in Figure 6-17 is kept. Following each practice the coach records the time spent at each drill, providing a basis of selection for drills in the next practice.

Without belaboring any of the basics, we will outline these drills, and, where needed, clarify some of the coaching points that we consider significant.

TACKLING DRILLS

Wide Butt Tackle (Figure 6-18)

The principles examined earlier in the text regarding Attitude Tackling apply to our tackling drills for defensive backs. The only difference between this drill and our normal Butt Tackling Drill is that we spread the bags 8-10 yards to provide a wider range, more closely simulating game conditions.

SCHEDULE OF DEFENSIVE BACKFIELD FUNDAMENTALS

DRILL	1st week	2nd week	etc.
TACKLING			
Wide Butt Tackling			
Sideline Tackling			
Balance Tackle Drill			
Tackleback Sled Tackling			
INDIVIDUAL			
Forty-fives with Partner			
Shuffle & Skate			
Competitive Skate Drill			
Interception Drill			
Tip Drill			
Combat Interception Drill			
Ball Reaction Drill			
Quick Cover Drill			
2-on-1 Zone Cover Drill			
Turn & Run Drill			
PAIRED DRILLS			
Seam Drill (Hb & Deep In)			
Square-out Drill (Hb & Up In)			
Crackback/Push Key Drill			
Lock-on Drill (Hb & Hawk)			
Level-off Drill (Hb & Hawk)			
PERIMETER DRILLS			
Pr. vs. 4 Lanes			
Pr. vs. Pass Patterns			
Pr. vs. Run on the Corner			

FIGURE 6-17

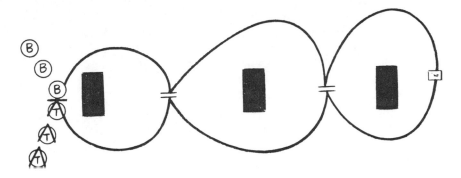

FIGURE 6-18

Sideline Tackling Drill (Figure 6-19)

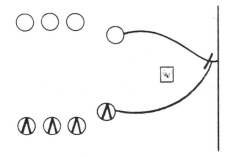

FIGURE 6-19

Learning to use the sideline as the "twelfth man" is as important to a defensive back as learning to hit. We concentrate on not overextending, getting the "head across the bow," and running through the ballcarrier.

Balance Tackle Drill As diagrammed and explained in Chapter 2 (Figure 2-7) the Balance Tackle Drill is basic to all players, but more than any others, we work the defensive backs regularly on this drill because they are the ones who will often find themselves approaching a ballcarrier directly in a 1-on-1 situation. We stress the need to come under control before going into the hit.

Tackleback Sled Tackling We like the way Gilman's Tackleback Sled requires good feet positioning. We use it often in the early season, and then again in the latter part of the week in-season. It can be an asset to building morale in practice, because there is a certain amount of ego lift that comes from wrestling that sled to the ground. It is just another way to build the player's self-confidence.

INDIVIDUAL PASS DEFENSE DRILLS

Forty-fives with a Partner (Figure 6-20)

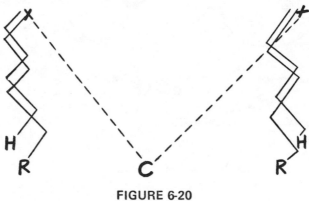

FIGURE 6-20

Work to keep the receiver in a position where you can play through him to the ball. Emphasis should be placed on rolling the hips as you open to one side and then the other. The receiver should be breaking off at 45° angles at 3/4 speed every 5 to 8 yards.

Shuffle and Skate (Figure 6-21)

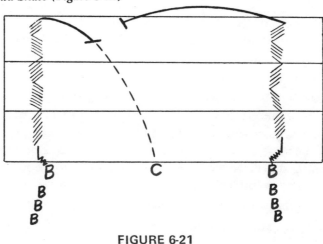

FIGURE 6-21

Maintain shoulders-over-the-toes posture while retreating to cover the deep pass. Following the shuffle, backpedal, then skate facing the direction that the coach points the ball. These should *not* be run on 45° angles, but the defender should maintain a path nearly parallel to the line of retreat. Throw ball a little short, between two defenders, to compare movement back into the ball. A man leaning back will not be able to recover as quickly.

The Competitive Skate Drill is the same, but have someone else throw ball and evaluate comparative abilities.

Interception Drill (Figure 6-22)

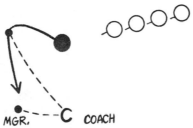

FIGURE 6-22

Vary the angle at which the receivers approach the pass. Concentrate on looking ball into hands and tucking it away. Defender should turn up field and give a burst of speed following each Hawk.

Tip Drill (Figure 6-23)

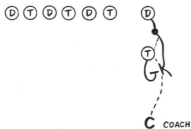

FIGURE 6-23

Ball should be thrown high and soft so that it can be tipped backward to defender. We like to have the tipper turn and be in position to butt the interceptor. This forces the defender to put the ball away securely before he begins to run.

Combat Interception Drill (Figure 6-24)

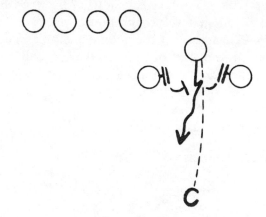

FIGURE 6-24

This is another way to insure that the defenders are concentrating on the ball, looking it into their hands and tucking it away immediately. The ball should be delivered high, just before the player enters the collision with the bags. We think this is the best drill for building concentration on the ball.

Ball Reaction Drill (Figure 6-25)

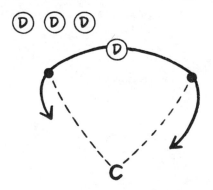

FIGURE 6-25

The defender breaks down and concentrates on the passer. As soon as the passer sets to throw, the defender breaks to that side, intercepts and returns the ball. This drill is often used as a two-minute introduction to the Quick Cover Drill.

Quick Cover Drill (Figure 6-26)

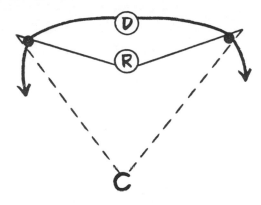

FIGURE 6-26

An excellent drill, combining reaction to movement, ball concentration and playing ball through the receiver. We even include this drill in our pre-game warm-ups. You can establish several variations to eliminate boredom, but it can't be overdone. (*Note:* Receiver's path must be slightly back, away from the passer.)

2-on-1 Zone Cover Drill (Figure 6-27)

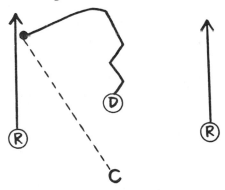

FIGURE 6-27

Common to all zone defense teams, this drill is the basis of all zone defensive principles. In the beginning, we start with a very narrow zone to cover and continually work toward widening it until it exceeds one-third of the field.

Turn and Run Drill (Figure 6-28)

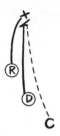

FIGURE 6-28

Some coaches might call it negative teaching to coach a boy on what to do *after* he has been beaten by the receiver, but we have taught our boys that they haven't been beaten until the opponent scores the TD. We tell our player to turn and run as fast as he can, keeping his eyes on the receiver. We say: "When the receiver looks up for the ball, if you are close enough, look up also, while extending both arms in the same direction as his. If you are not close enough, *don't lunge*, but continue running into the player so that you can hit him as soon after he receives the ball as possible. If you can prevent the TD on this play, our goal line defense will hold."

PAIRED DRILLS

The individual drills are the best way to develop the individual skills required for pass defense, but paired drills, isolating parts of the passing game, are the best way to go about developing good team pass defense.

Seam Drill (HB and Deep Invert) (Figure 6-29)

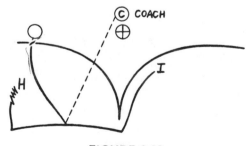

FIGURE 6-29

Moving from their original positions of alignment, the *deep* invert and HB close on their shared seam when reacting to the action of the passer. Drill should be varied to include HB and invert from same sides and from opposite sides.

Square-out Drill (HB and Up Invert) (Figure 6-30)

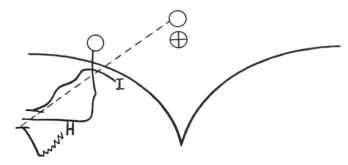

FIGURE 6-30

This drill should be worked in three stages: First, with no receiver, attempting to develop good area relationship; then, progressing to "bracketing" a single receiver on a square-out; and finally, having the invert picking up the second receiver as he enters the short zone.

Crackback or Push Key Drill (Figure 6-31)

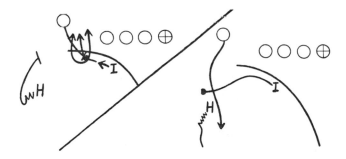

FIGURE 6-31

This drill is used to develop the confidence in the invert's ability to defeat the crackback block and to defend the flat zone against the pass. On the snap, the invert reacting *up* must look to his secondary key (the wide receiver), and read for crackback or push. If he reads *crackback*, he works to avoid the block and defends the corner. If he reads *push*, the wide-out releasing on a pass, he levels off as he did in the square-out drill. The halfback similarly reacts to cover pass or give secondary run support. *This is the single most important drill done by the defensive backs.* It is one in which the risk of body contact supersedes the cautions we all feel must be included in our drill work.

Additional paired drills such as the Level-Off and Bump and Run Technique Drills are more appropriate to our Hawk (5-man secondary) Defense and will be more appropriately discussed in that chapter.

PERIMETER DRILLS

Perimeter vs. 4 Lanes (Figure 6-32)

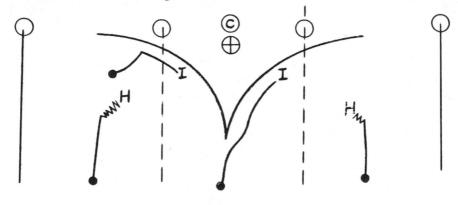

FIGURE 6-32

This is the logical extension of the 2-on-1 Zone Cover Drill. The four lanes represent the extents of the three deep zones, and should not be considered as receivers to cover but merely as the extreme points of responsibility. This drill should always be done on a fully lined field with the receivers running the sidelines and hashmarks. It can also be used to help the players understand the on-the-field significance of the concept of flexible zones discussed earlier. You can simply place the ball in strategic locations and show the players the extent of their responsibilities by placing receivers down each of the lanes established by the new ball position.

The second phase of perimeter drills comes in drilling against an opponent's particular passing attack and their outside running plays. Early in the season we'll have our offensive people run one type of play action at the corner each day, duplicating it to each side. For example, one day we'll defend against sprint-outs to a flanker, another day options to the weakside, etc.

We don't feel that we have any secret formula in the drills we have selected, but we do have them organized enough to make each one meaningful. The drills selected are progressive in nature, isolate skills involved in our assignments, and are easily adapted to our practice scheme. It is important, we believe, to keep records of what is being done, so that nothing is left to chance.

7

Utilizing the Fifth Defensive Back: Invert's Hawk Defense

Pro-type offenses place greater stress on the secondary than the more traditional sets, but their running game is more restricted, particularly to the split-end's side. The Hawk defensive alignment evolved because we found it to be a practical means of contending with the strong passing game and corner attack of the pro offense, without disrupting our basic invert secondary philosophy.

EVOLUTION OF THE HAWK CONCEPT

The basic 5-2 front of the Invert Defense is particularly effective against traditional tight formations because of the strength at the off-tackle area afforded by the variations of play by the end, tackle, linebacker and invert. When the end has been removed by the offense, however, their attack to that side is obviously limited, and it seems reasonable that the defense should also divert its strength to contend with the new-found potential of the offensive attack. We found that we too could remove a defender from the forcing unit without weakening ourselves. The fun came when we considered the possible ways we might incorporate this newly found Hawk into our defensive scheme. In our original Hawk alignment, we simply removed the tackle from the split-end's side (Figure 7-1), and brought the defensive end in to play over the split-side tackle. From this alignment we could, in effect, still loop right or left, stunt with all the variety normally used, and only commit ten men to the defense. Of course, our defensive halfback had to contend with a wide receiver as well as support the corner, but the important thing to us was that our forcing unit had not been weakened because both offense and defense had removed one player from the battle zone.

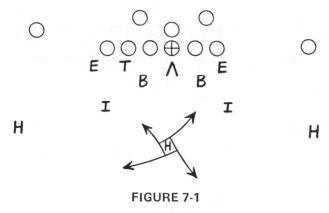

FIGURE 7-1

The Original Hawk Defense

Eventually, because of personnel and a desire for improved pass rush, we shifted the line to a balanced 4-2 alignment, but that came later; it is not permanent and it is far less exciting than the idea of having a fifth defensive back available. Later in the chapter, we'll return to our discussion of the forcing unit in the Hawk Defense, but for now, let us continue considering the multiple possibilities of utilizing the fifth back.

We considered many ideas regarding his placement, but the one we found most flexible and most valuable was to place the Hawk in the position of a safety, giving us the appearance of the balanced secondary in Figure 7-2.

From this balanced appearance we can predetermine double coverage to either side of the formation or field, achieve double coverage on movement of a key, lock-on into man-to-man coverage under a two-deep zone or simply vary the defense on the corner while maintaining stable zone secondary coverage. In effect, the secondary becomes two units functioning as one. The

Hawk and the two halfbacks function as a unit, while the inverts continue to play in tandem as they do in the normal Invert Defense.

LEVEL-OFF

To achieve double coverage on a particular receiver or to one side of the field, we can call a "level-right" or a "level-left." The

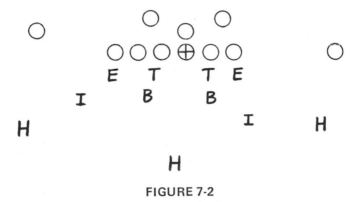

FIGURE 7-2

The Hawk Secondary

halfback to the side of the level call will rotate or "level off" into the short zone to that side, funneling the wide receiver to his inside. The Hawk will roll to the side of the level-off, assuming responsibility for the deep 1/3 to that side. Normal invert reaction will account for the placement of one invert coming to the deep middle while the other covers the flat or supports the corner.

Figure 7-3 represents a level-right call against a split-end to the wide side of the field on dropback pass action. Notice how the Hawk, right linebacker and right halfback function as a 3-on-2 group against the potential patterns of the split-end and near setback to the wide side, while the left halfback, left invert and linebacker zone the basic patterns to the formation strength. Except for the level-off technique of the halfback, no new techniques need be taught.

Sprint action toward the side of the level-off action permits the *up* invert to release from pass coverage and support the containment if the corner is truly being threatened, pick up a

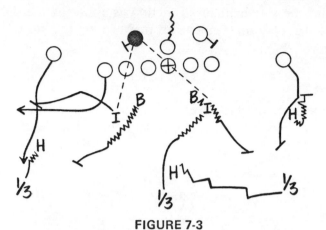

FIGURE 7-3

Level-Right vs. Dropback Pass

blocker who might be releasing late as a safety-valve receiver, or simply "squat" in the hole between the retreating linebacker and leveling halfback, reducing the width of each zone on that side. Figure 7-4 shows level-off action against the sprint-out.

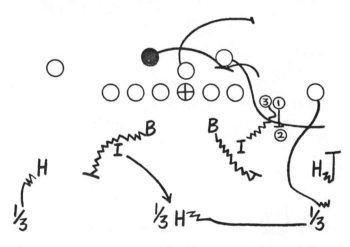

FIGURE 7-4

Sprint Action to the Level-off

While obviously strengthened to the side of the level-off, we are not really weakened away from the call, as normal invert action will bring us up into that flat on play action to that side or

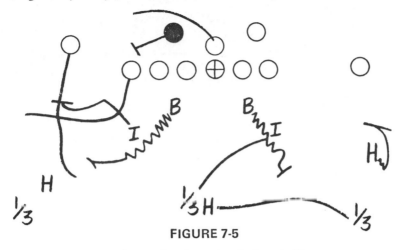

FIGURE 7-5

Sprint Action Opposite the Level-off

on straight dropback action, if there are two quick receivers to that side. Figure 7-5 shows the effect of sprint action opposite the side of a level-off.

There are four important coaching points that should be applied to teaching the level calls in the Hawk Defense. First is the halfback's technique in leveling. He should take his normal shuffle steps out and back, maintaining his original relationship with the receiver through his break off the line. On the third shuffle, he pushes off and shuffles forward, being sure to establish a position that will funnel the receiver to his inside. He concentrates through the receiver to the second potential receiver to his side. If that second receiver is in fact breaking out, the halfback picks him up; if he is not, the halfback brackets the wide receiver, taking away his sideline and turn-out cuts. He must always remember that he has help behind him.

Determining the Hawk's initial position is a second important point. He should be located midway between the two wide receiving threats or cheated slightly to the side of the level-off. He should be at least as deep from the ball as the widest receiver is split from the ball. His stance can be balanced or opened slightly either way, and on the snap he should open and sprint to the side, while looking over the inside shoulder (Figure 7-6).

When the invert is reacting *up* on the same side of the level-off, he must immediately decide if the corner is actually

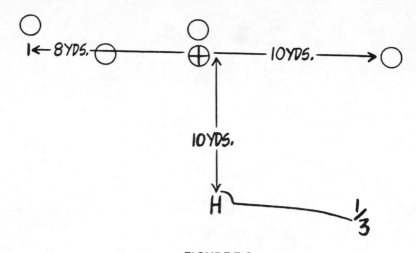

FIGURE 7-6

Hawk's Initial Position

being threatened. If it is, he will contain the QB without hesitation. If not, he should squat in the seam between the hook and flat, adding strength to our coverage on that side, while readying to attack the receiver who might be sliding out late. This situation requires drill work and complete understanding, but once achieved, results in a good percentage of interceptions (Figure 7-7).

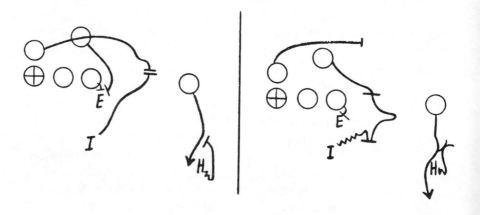

FIGURE 7-7

Invert "Squatting" vs. Sprint Action Pass

Finally, run responsibilities must be defined. No member of the secondary has any initial responsibility on a running play, or fake, inside of the tackles. Outside responsibility is unchanged from our normal defenses; that is, the invert should establish an inside-out leverage on the ball, knowing that the end's position will always be equivalent to that of an anchor end. The halfback, of course, is outside-in on the ball and can commit sooner if he is in a level-off position because he knows that he has help behind. The Hawk has no "fill" responsibility, and will not commit on a running play until the ball crosses the line of scrimmage.

HAWK KEYS

A call of Hawk keys combines the excellent corner defense of a level-off call with simpler deep coverage to straight dropback action. While selected keys can vary, the most common one would simply be the flow of the ball. On definite movement of the ball to one side of the formation, the halfback to that side would level off, the invert would react up and the Hawk would revolve to the deep outside, as shown in Figure 7-8.

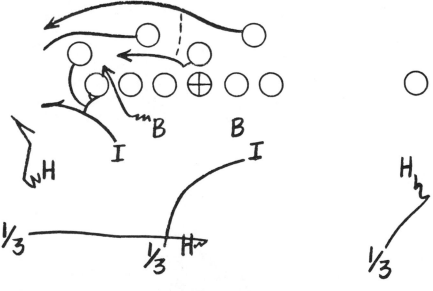

FIGURE 7-8

Hawk Keys vs. Flow

If flow was not established, as on straight drop action, the three deep would drop off to cover the three deep zones, while the inverts and linebackers covered the four short zones (Figure 7-9).

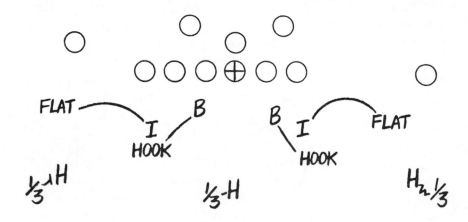

FIGURE 7-9

Hawk Keys vs. Dropback Action

One of the real strengths of the Hawk keys would be against a team that combines a solid passing attack with the Veer Option. We intend to take a more comprehensive look at defending this series in Chapter 10, but consideration of the basic strengths of Hawk keys against this play will show why we consider it to be basic to our total scheme of defense. The strongside option is neutralized by the inability of a tight end to effectively block the invert (Figure 7-10) and the level-off of the defensive halfback.

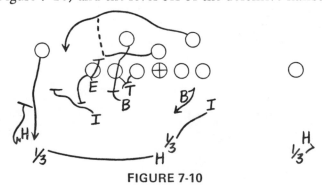

FIGURE 7-10

Hawk Keys vs. Strongside Veer Option

The weakside option is simply not a good call against this defense because of the defense's ability to flex its strength to that side, while offensively, no reversal of strength can be achieved. Figure 7-11 shows the weakside option.

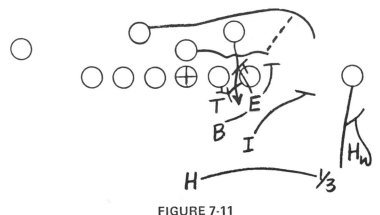

FIGURE 7-11

Weakside Veer Option vs. Hawk Keys

HAWK LOCK-ON

One of the most frustrating decisions a defensive coach must often make during the course of a game is whether to switch to a "prevent" defense late in a half or game, when the regular defensive calls have been doing so well. Inevitably, the opposing passer picks apart the zones underneath, and before you realize it you have your backs to the ball. We found the Hawk Lock-on to be the answer. With lock-on, or man-to-man, coverage underneath a two deep zone, we seemed to be more effective against the short pass without giving up much against the bomb.

Our approach was simple, so that regardless of the offensive set we all knew whom to cover, and who would assume responsibility for the deep zones. Basically, the halfbacks would lock-on the widest eligible receiver to their side. The Hawk would play deep-half to the two receiver side, the invert to that side would lock-on the tight end (or slot), and the opposite invert would cover the deep-half to his side. The linebackers would lock-on the setback to their side and cover hook to curl if they blocked (Figure 7-12).

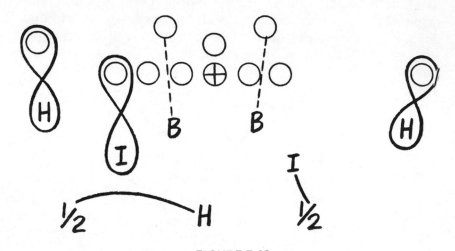

FIGURE 7-12

Hawk Lock-on vs. Pro Dropback Pass

Compensation for a set involving three quick receivers to the same side was the responsibility of the linebackers. Figure 7-13 shows the minor adjustment necessary to defend a triple receiver formation.

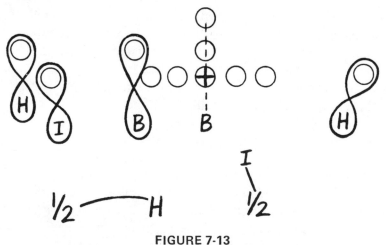

FIGURE 7-13

Hawk Lock-on vs. "Trips"

Lock-on coverage results in two new techniques that must be mastered by the defensive backs. If you are locking-on a split receiver we encourage the use of "bump and run" technique, a style that has become popular with many teams in the American Football Conference of the NFL. You line up just inside the receiver, about two yards off the ball with your inside foot forward. As the receiver releases, do not permit him to come inside of you, and as he closes the cushion between you, knock him out and back with your hands and arms and run with him. Concentrate on his eyes, and when he looks back for the ball, play the ball.

On a tight receiver, the above technique would be impractical. Instead, he must be played from outside in, and forced into the maze where a pass to him must be delivered over the rushing linemen.

THE HAWK FORCING UNIT

As indicated earlier in the chapter, a change was made in the play of our forcing unit in recent seasons. It is important to point out that this change was not made initially, although it was discussed, because we want our players to accept each variation of the total defense as an integral part of the whole. Our players were ready to accept the Hawk alignment diagrammed in Figure 7-1 as a valuable adjustment to our basic 5-2 alignment, because they could see how it was merely an extension of what we were doing already. When the personnel were available, and the Hawk Defense already an integral part of our total concept, the change was made to a balanced 4-2 front, without loops. It was sold to the players as a reward for being so good, as an opportunity to "whip" the man in front of you.

By this time we had decided that the Mikeman, middle guard, would be the player replaced by the Hawk. Our tackles had been asked to adjust as a Mike and tackle to the strong side, and the balanced alignment was simpler. They simply counted the number of tight linemen outside the center. If there were three, he clearly aligned outside the guard, while two tight linemen brought him in to a position head-up on the guard. Similarly, the defensive ends aligned head-on a tight end or on the outside shoulder of the tackle on the split side. The linebackers shaded the outside leg of the tackle as shown in Figure 7-14.

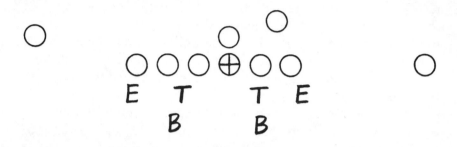

FIGURE 7-14

Alignment of Forcing Unit in Hawk Defense

Responsibilities of the front four were basic to the assignments of any similiar alignment. The tackles attacked through the guard's outside shoulder unless double-teamed by the tackle. They attempted to split the double-team, check the draw or attack the passer through the guard. The ends' first job was to contain the passer in the cup or pressure sprint action to their side. On a run, they were expected to close down the off-tackle hole, forcing the ball outside where the strength of the defense was located.

We feel that we were able to make the change to this balanced four-man front because we had four "studs" to play the positions, but we would not hesitate to return to the original Hawk alignment if our personnel were not strong enough to stand up and whip the man in front of them.

THE SCREAM'N HAWK

Having enjoyed some success with the four-man front, we considered using it as part of the forcing unit as a change of pace. We simply elected to move the Hawk up to the forcing unit as a true "monster" and play a balanced ten-man defense. We set up a series of stunts with the end, tackle and linebacker to the side of the Hawk. We now had a way to bridge the gap between the contain type of defenses we were using from the Hawk alignment and the pressure defenses associated with the fifty-front. Figure 7-15 shows the Scream'n Hawk alignment and basic stunts.

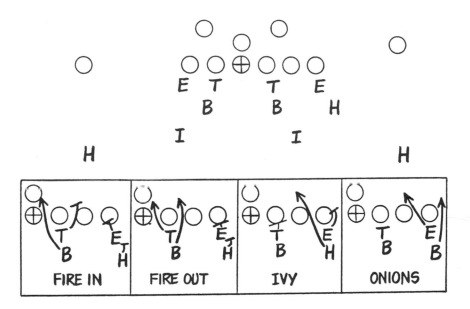

FIGURE 7-15

The Scream'n Hawk and Stunts

THE 4-3 FRONT

One season, injuries to two Mikemen and one tackle led to our acceptance of the 4-3 front into our basic scheme of defense. Our ends and tackles had shown they were capable of sitting in a four-man front, we had three good linebackers, and no adjustment at all was required by our secondary. A few simple rules were needed to establish alignment, and some basic decisions were necessary on how linebackers would react to flow. Once determined, a new facet of River Dell's Invert Defense became a reality.

The tackle's alignment was the same as in the Hawk defense, and the middle linebacker obviously aligned in the middle. The end to the side of a tight end aligned to his outside with the linebacker shading the tight end's inside, while on the split-end side, the end would move into the outside shoulder of the tackle and the linebacker would be a yard out and back (Figure 7-16).

As a basic adjustment, we decided to have the outside linebacker to the side of flow, fire or pressure the play, while the

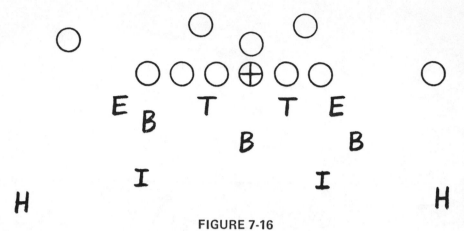

FIGURE 7-16

Basic 4-3 Invert Alignment

middle linebacker scraped and covered that hook zone. On dropback action we asked the middle linebacker to check draw and then pressure the passer through any available seam. We included two alternatives to the basic coverage, a "Cover" call from which all three linebackers dropped, and a "Fire" call predetermining a fire for one of the three backers.

A CAUTION TO THE READER

When you have completed reading this chapter, unless you were previously familiar with the Invert Defense as employed at River Dell High School your head is probably ringing, and that negative feeling—"We couldn't do all that"—is creeping into your mind. The fact is that we have done all that was unfolded on these pages, but only a little at a time and only when necessary. It is basic to our philosophy that multiple variations and adjustments can be made in the forcing unit from week to week without problem, but that adjustments in the secondary must be well thought out and prepared for. The Hawk Defense might not be used by us for two or three games, and then show up as the basic defense for another game. The important thing is that our kids recognize that it is merely an adjustment of our total concept of defense, a segment that will be most advantageous to us in that particular game.

It is the coach's responsibility to understand the value and use of the tools that he has available to him. The flexibility of the Invert Defense is one of its greatest values. The important task for the coach is recognizing when it will be to his advantage to reach into his bag of tricks for a segment of the Hawk or 4-3 defense. The recipe for success is built on basics and spiced with variations to taste.

8

Using the Invert
on Goal Line and Short Yardage

Goal-line and short-yardage situations dictate a definite need for adjustments in the defensive scheme, without conflicting with the overall defensive philosophy. Accepting the fact that our opponent will at times maneuver us into the position of defending our goal line is the first step toward achieving success in this critical area. Confidence and pride are the two most important qualities of sound goal-line and short-yardage defense.

EVOLUTION OF OUR GOAL-LINE PHILOSOPHY

As we did in developing the Hawk Concept (Chapter 7), we sought to extend our basic defensive philosophy to meet the specific needs presented by a unique field position—the down-and-distance situation. Traditionally, the short-yardage or goal-line play was met with a gap-8 or pinching-7 or six-man front. The general feeling of most coaches was that this was no place to stunt; you lined up and attacked the offense, closing all available line splits.

As scouting and game planning became more sophisticated, however, the need to vary the direction of defensive charge paralleled the offensive team's potential for attacking a hole with several different blocking schemes. If the offense knew exactly where you would be, it was easy to establish a goal-line offense that could attack anywhere along the line, using isolation or option blocking.

Initially, we felt that we could retain our basic 5-2 alignment on the goal line and simply cheat our inverts up a little more toward the line. From that alignment we could slant the line in one direction, while scraping off and filling with the inverts and one linebacker against the grain. Figure 8-1 shows our original Goal-Line Monster call which could be mirrored by Goal-Line Chuckles, giving us two different ways to fill all the gaps and attack the offense. This approach proved very successful for us because it filled the gaps, forced offensive blockers to guess regarding their assignments and, most importantly, it conformed to our total defensive scheme. Our players could feel comfortable and confident in it.

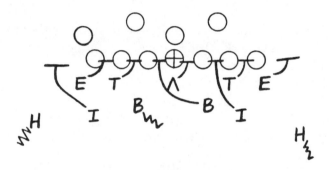

FIGURE 8-1

Original "Goal-Line Monster

After the Invert Defense had been in use for several seasons, we reached the point as a coaching staff where we could isolate segments of total defense and refine them individually, without causing the players to question or lose confidence in what we were doing. The only real weakness that had shown with any degree of consistency was the inability of our linebacker to fill quickly enough against a QB sneak opposite the loop of the Mikeman. As we considered possible solutions to this single problem, we developed a comprehensive concept of the demands of goal-line and short-yardage defense. We reviewed our own offensive thinking on the goal line and what we had encountered from our opponents. We decided that there were actually three distinctly different goal-line situations, each requiring something slightly different from the defense.

THREE LEVELS OF GOAL-LINE PLAY

To solve our initial problem of contending with the QB sneak, without diverging from our basic defensive philosophy, we elected to align in a 6-5, with the only change being the substitution of a strong down-lineman for the weaker of our two linebackers. Regardless of the down and distance on a goal-line play we would always show the same basic 6-5 alignment (Figure 8-2). However, a different call would be used in each of the three general goal-line situations. We like to use the Rush Defense on short-yardage plays out on the open field—on 3rd and 1 at the fifty, for example. It is extremely effective against a wedge or delayed middle play, while maintaining adequate containment and good pass defense. On the goal line, Rush is reserved for situations in which the offense must average more than four yards on each remaining down. On 3rd and goal from the ten, we are looking for a pass, option or counter-action play, and we believe that the Rush call will be the strongest and safest.

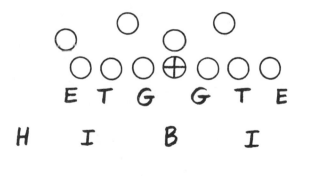

FIGURE 8-2

Goal-Line and Short-Yardage Alignment

Under normal goal-line conditions, an offensive play must average from two to four yards for a scoring drive to be successful. Our philosophy in this instance is the same as our philosophy on the rest of the field: "Force a mistake." Our Goal-Line Monster and Goal-Line Chuckles calls have been cast in that mold. They are aggressive, stunting variations of the basic look, intended to cause a fumble or create a long-yardage situation. Finally, there are times when the obvious advantage is with the offense. When they can score by averaging less than two yards per play, the advantage is clearly theirs, and nothing less than a total commitment by the defense will suffice. Goal-Line Pride is our call for this situation, and it amounts to attacking the offense. Under counterattack by the defense, an offense is as likely to err as it is to score. Psychologically, it really doesn't matter whether they score in one play or three from the two-yard line, but a mishandled ball will completely reverse the momentum of the occasion.

The Defensive Captain's rules for goal-line and short-yardage calls are summarized on his defensive call sheet (Figure 5-4). Each player has been completely schooled in our goal-line philosophy, as well as subjected to overwhelming propaganda regarding our success in this area in the past. We make it a point to devote a period of a pre-season scrimmage, against a team we consider to be weaker, to goal-line offense and defense. We will mentally prepare our players for this small aspect of the scrimmage because we want them "oozing with confidence" about their ability to play goal-line defense. We try to convince our players that there is not a single opponent who puts the time and effort into goal-line offense that we put into goal-line defense. We believe that the advantage is truly ours in this area, and that in addition to preventing a score, we will reverse the game's momentum with our play in this area. Our players understand that our goal-line defense is team defense, and that it is not simply a test of standing up under assault, but is our most offensive level of defense.

CLOSING OFF THE MIDDLE

There is no deception in the play of our defensive guards on any of the goal-line calls. Their responsibility is to seal off the offensive middle, but their technique will vary with the call. On a Rush call, for example, in the goal-line area, the guards will each align on the inside shoulder of the offensive guard (Figure 8-3) and be sure to take their initial step with the outside foot, stepping up into the guard's block. They do not seek to penetrate excessively, but merely to occupy this inside area, looking for delayed action up the middle, and being satisfied with stopping the edge or sneak for a short gain.

FIGURE 8-3

Guard Play on a Rush Call

It must be remembered that if the Rush defense is being used on the goal line, we have already achieved the long-yardage situation we are striving for. If Rush is called on a short-yardage situation in the mid-field area, the guards are free to determine how wide they will play on the basis of scouting information and the actual distance required. If it were 4th and less than a foot, their play would more closely resemble what would be expected of them on a Goal-Line Pride call.

On a normal goal-line situation, when Goal-Line Monster or Chuckles would be the call, the guards will actually align in the center-guard gap, and depending on the size of the split taken by the offensive guard will either shoot the gap, attack out into the guard or pinch to the near leg of the QB (Figure 8-4). We want the guard's charge to be balanced and wide enough so that he can not be cut off by a center's reach block. The center can only support to one side, and the other guard then controls this rather congested area. The most important consideration of the guards in this situation is the wedge or quick sneak by the QB.

FIGURE 8-4

Guard Play on Goal-Line Mon-Chuckles

On the Goal-Line Pride call, the guards are expected to align with a piece of the center's blocking surface. We don't want them pinching down to the center, but rather attacking the center straight on, shoulder to shoulder, neutralizing his forward progress, and then being able to slide off him to their own side. Both men must blow off the ball, establishing an initial point of contact under the center's blocking surface and then lifting (Figure 8-5).

FIGURE 8-5

Guard Play on Goal-Line Pride

THE RUSH DEFENSE

As indicated, the Rush call is used on the goal line after the long-yardage situation has been created. We are primarily concerned with defending the short passing game, which we feel we can do best with man-to-man coverage, and funneling the ball to the inside, where our four biggest players are controlling the area. The alignment for the Rush Defense is the same as for all goal-line calls (Figure 8-6).

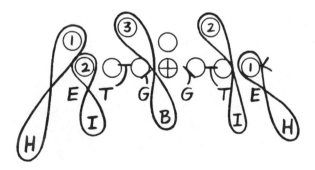

FIGURE 8-6

Rush Defense

The play of the guards has already been described and diagrammed in Figure 8-3. They should be principally concerned with controlling the area, and should not anxiously pursue, but look for counters.

Both tackles are on an inside loop, and the basic fundamentals that apply normally to their play are still in practice. If the guard is pulling away from him, as often is the case of a goal-line blocking scheme, the tackle must avoid the cutoff block and get in that guard's pocket. That pulling guard is often the key blocker on an outside play in the goal-line area, the play we are very concerned with. On drop-back pass, both guard and tackle are attacking the offensive guard, providing the tackle with what should be the most advantageous route to the passer. One caution must be recognized in this instance, and that is that the tackle must avoid being ridden down the line by the down block on the offensive tackle. If ball movement is toward him and blocking is solid to his side, he must be able to penetrate or spin off the tackle's block. As we will show shortly in this discussion, we are, in fact, encouraging the offense to run in the off-tackle area in this down and distance situation on the goal-line.

Defensive end play on the Rush is basically the same as a Loop End; that is, he has immediate contain responsibility. We do not want him running around a blocker, but it is important that he not allow himself to be hooked. By limiting his initial penetration, he will reduce the off-tackle running lane while maintaining his contain responsibility.

In effect, the six-man front has controlled the running game of the offense by closing off the inside and establishing a definite contain on the ball. The off-tackle running lane must then be filled by the five-man secondary.

Responsibilities in the secondary are clear and simple. Each defender has man-to-man responsibility on pass, and run support as dictated by the movement of their key. The halfbacks are responsible for the widest eligible receiver to their side. If the key blocks on play action to their side, they should support the corner. The invett is man to man on the second widest receiver to their side, normally a tight end, slotback or setback. If the key blocks they will fill, normally off-tackle, unless it is clearly outside and containment is threatened. If their key goes away (during the play), they can drop off toward the middle. The middle linebacker is responsible for the third potential receiver to either side, normally the fullback. He will fill the off-tackle hole on flow to either side, play zone if the key pass blocks or maintain leverage on the passer and blocker if the QB rolls toward either side.

Man-to-man coverage involves certain basic problems in adjustment to formations and motions. We have no foolproof solution for them; we simply attempt to enforce the 1-2-3 receiver responsibility according to position of receivers at the snap of the ball. Occasionally this will involve a minimum of shuffling to maintain leverage on a receiver, but under no circumstances do we want one football player running across the field chasing another. We prefer to switch or shift responsibility when it is called for.

If the offensive coach were given the chalk last, we predict that he would attempt to attack our Rush Defense with crossing pass patterns, which tend to take longer and are difficult to throw if you are attacking a corner, and the Off-Tackle Power Play. Figure 8-7 shows the Rush Defense vs. the Off-Tackle Power.

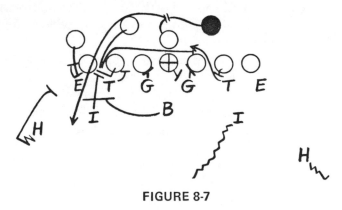

FIGURE 8-7

Rush Defense vs. Off-Tackle Power

GOAL-LINE MONSTER AND CHUCKLES

Goal-Line Monster or Chuckles is the normal goal-line call. The most important characteristic of either call is that they are designed to "cause an offensive error." The only difference between our Goal-Line Monster today (Figure 8-8) and the original form diagrammed in Figure 8-1 is the play of the guards from the six-man front, rather than firing a linebacker from the five.

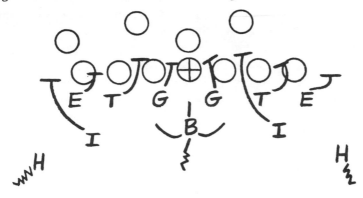

FIGURE 8-8

Goal-Line Monster

The big play maker in the Goal-Line Monster has traditionally been the right invert firing the offensive guard-tackle gap. As is obvious from the diagram, the commitment of both inverts, along with the six-man line, places us ultimately into a "gap-8," with the major difference being that the offense does not see us sitting in that position before the play begins. The Goal-Line Chuckles is simply a mirror of the Monster call, with a similar end result, but with gaps being filled from the opposite positions.

Goal-Line Chuckles is diagrammed below in Figure 8-9; the coaching points discussed for it would naturally apply for the Goal-Line Monster call.

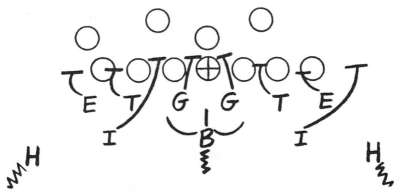

FIGURE 8-9

Goal-Line Chuckles

With the area between the guards controlled by our defensive guards and supported by the middle linebacker, maximum attention is given to the dive hole and off-tackle areas, the holes most likely to be attacked in a normal goal-line situation. On the defensive right, these holes are being filled by the inside movement of the tackle and defensive end, while the firing invert and loop tackle are filling them on the left side. The important thing is that they are being filled, and it is impossible to predict on the basis of scouting whether the dive hole, for example, will be filled by a tackle or an invert. It is this moment of indecision by the offensive blockers that transfers the advantage from the offense to the defense in this critical area.

An anchor end closes hard in the off-tackle area, consciously aware of the possible sliding off of a ballcarrier stopped in the congested middle. The loop end assumes responsibility for the flat, pitchman on an option and containing the sweep. The right invert, moving up onto the corner, has the same responsibilities as the end looping out of the other side. Looking at the entire defensive front, we see that eight men have been committed across the front, each basically responsible for a gap.

The most obvious weakness of the call is the inability to defend the "seam" on play-action passes to the tight end. While the halfbacks are usually sound against passes to the outside, it is difficult for an aggressive middle linebacker to show restraint on play-action and adequately defend the pass to the short-middle or play-side seam. We accept this limitation, and contend that *most* football teams when presented with a "normal" goal-line situation will not go to play-action passes to the inside. It is the coach's responsibility to recognize the team that will go to that type of play, and call "Rush" in that instance. Back in our General Defensive Philosophy (Chapter 5), we said that anticipation of a particular play would primarily dictate the defensive call. Goal-Line Monster and Goal-Line Chuckles are, we feel, the best calls against the basic goal-line offensive attacks.

GOAL-LINE PRIDE

The third and final level of goal-line defense is reserved for the most vital of situations. When an opponent can score while averaging less than two yards a carry, you can almost bet that they are not going to fool around with any misdirection or fancy ball handling. They are going to come at you with power, and to stop them, you must attack them with power, as diagrammed in Figure 8-10, Goal-Line Pride.

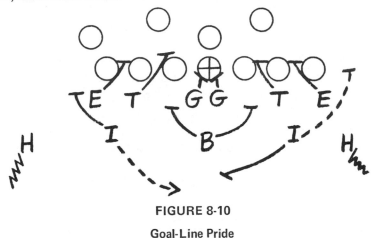

FIGURE 8-10

Goal-Line Pride

There are two important coaching points in teaching the line play for this call. First the guards, as discussed earlier, must each get a piece of the center, lifting him and neutralizing his forward progress in order to stop the advancement of the ball by the quarterback or fullback. And second, we ask our tackles and ends to utilize a different technique in closing down to the inside. Whereas we normally step with the inside foot and dip the trail shoulder on a scoop movement to avoid the offensive blocker's blow, we now ask him to step across with the far foot, insuring quicker contact with the blocker and definite movement to the inside while producing immediate congestion in the hole. We have found that this technique when used by the tackles and ends is more effective in closing the inside gaps against power thrusts, and the only thing that is lost from the normal technique is the ability to pursue opposite the slant, which is of little value in this situation.

The halfbacks are the only players showing any caution at all, as they assume responsibility for the outside and will remain at home on action away from them, looking for reverse or throwback pass. The middle linebacker fires hard on flow to the ball or off-tackle hole (first opening), while on flow to an invert he will commit into the flat to contain the ball; the invert away from flow will commit to the middle, looking for a cutback or inside counter.

DEVELOPING CONFIDENCE IN GOAL-LINE DEFENSE

At the beginning of this chapter we indicated that confidence and pride were the two most important aspects of successful goal-line defense. Building that confidence is not isolated in any single exercise or procedure, but is an intregal part of our total coaching process. We feel that we have developed a comprehensive approach to defending this region, and that our players understand it and believe in it.

Through the years we have tried several different methods of building and mantaining awareness of goal-line situations. It is easy to use the charts of a successful season to support the importance of good goal-line play because they will always show that the winner is statistically the team with the advantage in this region. Other methods are equally desirable, and should be used if your past performance doesn't measure up to what you consider to be acceptable standards. Charting all goal-line situations as they evolve through a season is an excellent way of building pride in a new program, as well as maintaining awareness of the importance of goal-line play. A training film of successful goal-line stands is also a valuable coaching aid, as it will build confidence in your goal-line calls.

It has been common for us to make two changes in personnel when shifting into the goal-line defense, replacing the Mikeman and one linebacker with two stronger interior linemen. Aside from the obvious advantage of this substitution—providing two players better equipped physically to handle the goal-line guard assignments—there is an important psychological advantage. These players represent a signal to the rest of the defense that gives it a lift, an indication that we are now physically and mentally prepared to reverse the momentum of the game and prove once and for all that we are the best.

9

Coordinating the Kicking Game
with Invert Defense

We could not consider a discussion of defensive football to be complete without including our thoughts on the kicking game. In our scheme of things, the offense takes over when the ball has been awarded to them by the defense in the best possible field position. When one of our backs returns a punt for a score, we don't want it thought of as an offensive score: that's our touchdown, earned by the defense and *scored* by the defense! Similarly, when our offense has had the ball and failed to drive for a score, the punting team is a *defensive* team, whose responsibility is to regain field position and, ultimately, ball control.

THE KICKING GAME PHILOSOPHY—THE MARGIN OF VICTORY

The biggest victories each year are most often the close ones, and in each, we all look for something to give us the margin of victory. An offensive back or receiver gaining over 100 yards in one game would immediately be recognized for his achievements; however, in the exchange of seven or eight punts during the course of a typical game, one team can quite often gain over a 100-yard advantage with little recognition. One hundred yards is just as important on a punt exchange as it is when run from scrimmage, and we have to communicate this emphatically to the players.

Our statistics indicate that over 50 percent of all offensive drives beginning behind midfield will end up as a punt. If this is true for both teams in an equally matched game, a real offensive advantage can be earned by the team that gains the "hidden yardage" of the exchange of kicks. To bring this to the players' attention we employ three basic approaches: (1) a defined Kicking Period of ten minutes, regularly scheduled in the middle of our practice; (2) a Kicking Game Bulletin Board, which shares equal status with the Offensive and Defensive Boards; and (3) a complete Kicking Game Manual, as detailed and important as its offensive and defensive counterparts.

We had tried in earlier years to include offensive punting in the offensive teamwork period, and punt returns in our defensive teamwork period, but were plagued by several problems. First, as mentioned earlier, we really consider our punting team to be a defensive team. We really didn't like finishing group work with punting because it was a negative approach. We prefer to work our offense toward the goal line in teamwork, developing a pattern of general plays followed by special field positions, and, ultimately, emphasizing scoring on the goal line, pressuring to victory. We like to include many of the younger players in various aspects of our "special teams," and we would always have to go hunt them down from JV or soph groups to participate in this phase of practice. Similarly, we like to finish defensive teamwork with either goal-line, prevent, or some other special phase of our defensive game plan. By using the kicking game as a buffer between fundamentals and teamwork, it gains the special recognition it deserves, provides a mid-practice meeting ground for the entire squad, and can easily be adapted to include all phases of the kicking game without being out of place.

It is important to have a seasonal schedule to practice the kicking game. During each pre-season practice, for example, the entire period will be devoted to a single phase: i.e., punt returns, kickoffs, extra points. As the season moves closer, we employ the punt and punt returns with greater regularity. By early season we are able to employ several phases in each early week practice, and the entire kicking game will be reviewed every Thursday and Friday.

THE KICKING GAME BULLETIN BOARD

The JV/Soph Defensive Coach assumes responsibility for the Kicking Game Board. As previously mentioned, it shares equal status with its offensive and defensive counterparts, and is a station of buzzing interest soon after it is posted each Monday. Basically it consists of three major parts, and it is quite easy to keep up to date. The biggest attention getter from the team's viewpoint is the Kicking Game "Advantage Chart" which maintains top-center position on the board. Individually, interest is centered on the "Specialists," where recognition is given to each of the players who have made tackles, kicked or returned kicks. Along each side of the board are individual charts showing our success and that of our opponents in each aspect of the kicking game (Figure 9-1).

The Kicking Game "Advantage" is computed by taking the net advancement (punt minus the return) for all kicks by each team and comparing the totals. In general, the total number of punts plus kickoffs by each team will be nearly equal, as the reduced number of punts by the winning team in a lopsided game will be offset by more kickoffs following each touchdown.

The enlarged diagram of the Kicking Advantage Chart (Figure 9-2) shows the results of a game in which we punted four times for 140 yards minus 5 return yards, and kicked off four times (195-50) for a net of 145 yards and a total of 280 yards. Our opponent punted six times for a net of 160 yards (200-40) and kicked off once for (50-20) 30 net yards and a total of 190 yards, giving us a 90-yard advantage in the hidden yards of the kicking game that day.

The form used to represent graphically what happened on both opponent and River Dell kickoff and punt returns is the same. Each kick is shown on its relative position on the field, from origin of the kick to beginning of return, and the result of the return. If it is a River Dell return, the ballcarrier's name is shown. On opponent returns, the tackler's name is shown. On rare occasions, we have added the names of particular blockers, pointing out the key blocks that they might have made in a long or touchdown return (Figure 9-3).

On the Extra Point Charts, we simply list each extra point attempted in the game, how it was executed and the result. At the bottom of the chart, we compile the success ratio of both one- and two-point conversion attempts for the season.

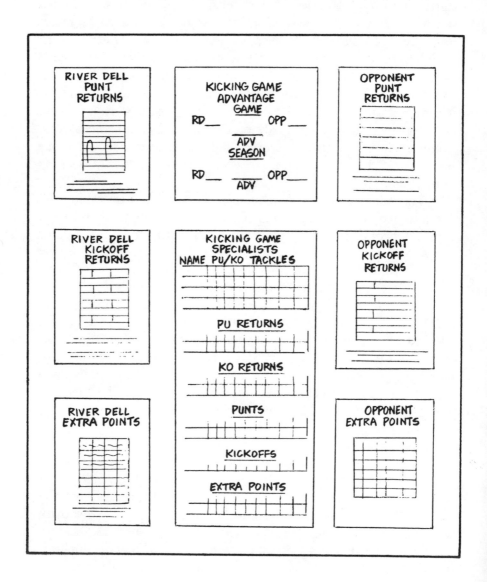

FIGURE 9-1

The Kicking Game Bulletin Board

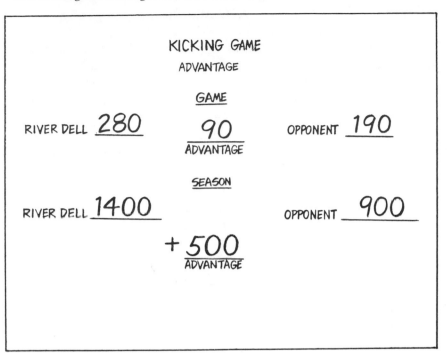

FIGURE 9-2

Kicking Game Advantage Chart

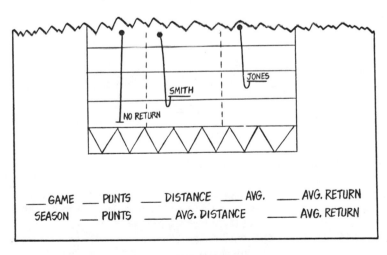

FIGURE 9-3

Opponent Punt Returns

Each of our kicking teams is made up of specialists, and a conscious effort is made to mix in those younger athletes who show potential to be regulars in the future. Year in and year out, we have found the leading tackler in the kicking game to be not a regular performer, but a sophomore or "fringe" senior who makes up his mind that this will be his claim to fame. We encourage boys with the opportunity to break into the line-up this way.

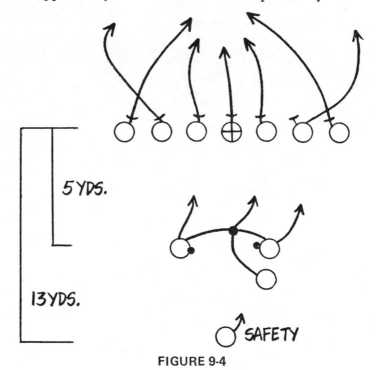

FIGURE 9-4

The Spread Punt Formation

Spread Punt Blocking and Coverage Rules

FRONT LINE — (all)	*HIM BLOCK*, that is, fire directly into the man on your inside gap or head-on. Neutralize his charge and pick up your coverage lane.
WIDEST MEN —	On release, go directly at the receiver's outside shoulder. If the ball hasn't arrived yet as you approach, "choke your motor" and watch his eyes. *Don't look back for the ball.*

SECOND MAN IN — (tackles)	Hit, release outside, *contain.*
GUARDS —	Hold your block a moment longer, then cover. If you sense a wall forming, go toward that side, crowd the blockers as they are setting up.
CENTER —	*Make a perfect snap*, block or be blocked, cover.
BIG "3" —	*Protect the kicker*, don't step back, don't chase to block. If they don't come *through* you, they can't block the kick. Cover to your side.

We like to place our three biggest "good" linemen back in the big three. When we found one season that our best center for punts was also the best punter, we kept him at center. The elimination of one bad snap is worth more than a few extra yards on all of the punts. In the front line, we expect our widest men to have exceptional speed, and the second men in (tackles) have traditionally been defensive ends.

We spend very little time teaching the Tight Punt, but do have it as a part of our plan if we are backed up to the goal line. It is the traditional tight punt with shoe-to-shoe linemen and two blockers to the backfield side of the kicker's foot. The kicker is ten yards back when he receives the snap from center. (Figure 9-5 shows our Tight Punt Formation.)

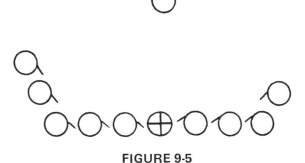

FIGURE 9-5

Tight Punt Formation

Our basic conservative nature precludes our extensive use of a run-from-punt formation, but we include it in our Manual to use perhaps once a season against a team that shows in scouting a real tendency to peel off to one side or the other when forming a wall (Figure 9-6).

FIGURE 9-6

Run from Punt Formation

Our punt formation, with three big men back, does not lend itself well to passing. Most defenses have at least two backs positioned to take away the initial passing threat to their side. We have enjoyed some success by starting out with a run toward the short side, often opposite most returns, turning the receiver to that side out at the "stake" and running the other end across on a drag pattern behind the linebackers (Figure 9-7).

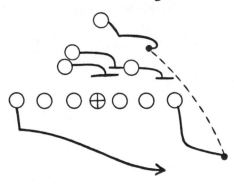

FIGURE 9-7

Punt Formation Pass

We "quick kick" several times each season from our basic "I" formation. The QB pitches the ball back to the kicker, who uses a side-type of kick to produce a long, low, hard-driving kick. We have even used motion to get our slotback in position to kick if we determined that he had the best foot, but that tends to loosen the secondary a little before the snap. We believe that the Quick Kick is essential to good defensive football.

Punt Returns There are probably as many minor variations of a basic theme employed in punt returns as in any other aspect of football. We believe in keeping it simple so that many players can learn the rules, because each week there are likely to be several changes in the punt return line-up. Our basic return, Punt Return Right or Left, is diagrammed in Figure 9-8.

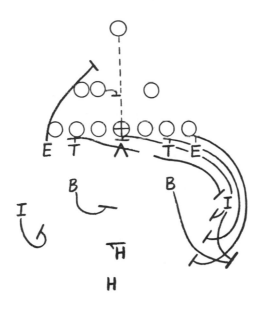

FIGURE 9-8

Punt Return Right

Blocking Rules:

LEFT END:	Rush kicker hard, block or force immediate kick. Continue path across formation and pick up block.
TACKLES:	Deliver blow on offensive tackle, hold up his release as you check run, peel off line to form wall.
MIKE:	Attack center, check run and peel off to form wall.
RIGHT END:	Deliver blow on end, check run, peel off to start wall. Set up at depth determined by length of kick.
LEFT LB:	Check run and pass, block first man releasing up middle.
RIGHT LB:	Check run and pass, double-team first man to show on right outside with right invert.
LEFT INVERT:	Check pass, block first down your side.
RIGHT INVERT:	Check pass, double-team first man with LB.
UP HALFBACK:	Personal protector for return man.

We often like to use a middle return against a team that is not well disciplined in the kicking game. If we have one outstanding return man, we simply try to set him up by providing him with a little room straight ahead, and then put him on his own (Figure 9-9).

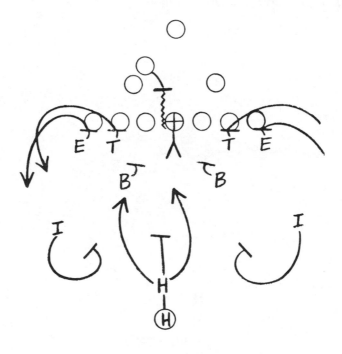

FIGURE 9-9

Middle Punt Return

We try to carry the aggressive nature of our defensive game into punt return team by employing, and working hard on, an effective punt rush, "Bullets." The diagram, Figure 9-10, indicates that we like to employ an outside rush to the punter to reduce the chance for "roughing." We will make minor variations in the positions of our stacks according to the punt formation and personnel we are aligned against.

Extra Points and Field Goals On our field goal and extra point attempts, our offensive line anchors their outside foot and turns in toward the center (Figure 9-11).

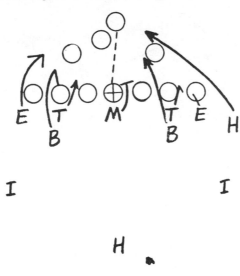

FIGURE 9-10

"Bullets," the Punt Rush

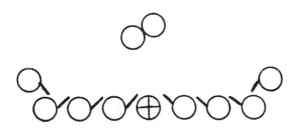

FIGURE 9-11

Field Goal Alignment

Defending the extra point or field goal is one aspect of the game often left to chance, but the fact is that a big play during one of those kicking attempts can neutralize an awful lot of big plays during a scoring drive. Our field goal defenses stem from our Goal Line 65 alignment. We have three levels of play for the field goal: FG Block, FG Cover and FG Return. The use of each in our game plan is obvious, and all of them are practiced. Figure 9-12 shows each of them.

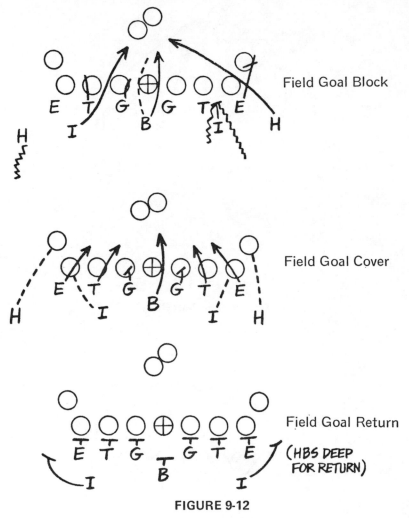

Field Goal Block

Field Goal Cover

Field Goal Return

(HBS DEEP FOR RETURN)

FIGURE 9-12

Field Goal Defenses

Kickoffs and Kickoff Returns Our kickoff coverage is simple and well defined. It is designed that way so that continuous changes of personnel that make up the unit each week will not cause mistakes. We have eight men closing on the ball as quickly as possible. The closer they are to the middle, the slower they can be, and the stronger they must be. Our outside men must have speed and courage; the next ones, our contain men, are often defensive ends. Figure 9-13 shows our kickoff coverage, and Figure 9-14 shows our onside kick.

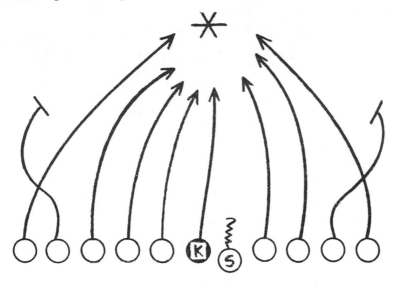

FIGURE 9-13

Kickoff Coverage

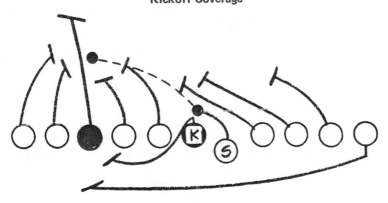

FIGURE 9-14

Onside Kick

We like to practice extra hard on one kickoff return each week. We expect to be returning one kickoff every week (opener or half-time), and occasionally two, but rarely more than that. Thus we can pick from our scouting report the return that we feel is best suited for that week and practice hard on it. We have three returns, each starting out the same way and each having simple blocking rules. Figure 9-15 shows our kickoff returns.

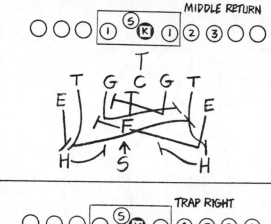

MIDDLE RETURN

BLOCKING RULES

Center—Attack kicker

Gds—Cross trap #1 (ignore safety, rt in front of lt)

Tackles—Turnout #3

Ends—Cross trap #2 (rt in front of lt)

FB—Lead up middle

Backs—Return up middle, get in front of ball, *block and run*

TRAP RIGHT

BLOCKING RULES

Center and Gds—Block *core*, same as middle return.

Rt Tackle—Double with end on #3

Lt Tackle—Lead on #4.

Rt End—Double #3

Lt End—Lead

FB—Trap #2 (if cross trap #1, ignore wide)

Backs—Start up middle, cut out behind double team.

TRAP LEFT

Same as return right but mirrored. Double team 3rd man in from outside, FB trap #2 man, offside end and tackle lead, middle three block the core.

FIGURE 9-15

Kickoff Returns

10

Invert Defense vs.
the "Offense of the Seventies"

To suggest that a single offensive pattern will characterize the Seventies shows little respect for the individuality of thousands of outstanding coaches on the high school level in the United States. While football coaches may be the greatest copycats in the world, they always incorporate so many of their own basic ideas into any system that the end result is unique and requires individual defensive attention.

THE OFFENSE OF THE SEVENTIES

On the first page of this book, we suggested that high school coaches saw two tight ends and a wingback in 90 percent of their games. That was basically true in the Sixties, but in the present decade the trend is definitely away from that. Pro style "pitch and catch" football has been fed to our young players by television, newspapers and armchair quarterbacks everywhere. Passing game skills have been developed by more players at a younger age than ever before. Summer football camps, for example, have isolated the passing game as an aspect of football easily taught under pleasant camp conditions. The successful high school football coach will capitalize on all of this by opening up his traditional offense to appeal to the young men who have developed these special skills. To the Defensive Coach, this means that he will have to take a closer look at "multiple coverages." College and Pro coaches have prophesied for some time now that a single type of zone or man coverage is not sufficient, and that several coverage schemes must be integrated into the total defensive package.

Just as the Pros have influenced the high school game, the Veer Option of college football is also having its effect. The endless variety of ways that college teams have found to incorporate this series into their offenses is indicative of its strong appeal. Certainly, the Wishbone formation as popularized by Texas, Oklahoma and Alabama appears to be the "set" which will initially gain acceptance by the high school coaches. There are two main reasons, in addition to its success, for this. First, a great deal of well-documented information is available on the Wishbone in the form of books, articles, the Texas Wishbone film, and even college classroom seminars, such as Jim Brakefield's at Appalachian State University in North Carolina. Second, the Wishbone is mutually satisfying to the tradition-oriented coaches, who will reluctantly release one wide-out from the formation, and the "modern" player who is satisfied by its popular appeal. The Wishbone set and Veer Option present particular problems to the defense which must be considered as paramount in successful defensive planning for the "Defense of the Seventies."

A third important characteristic of the offense we anticipate seeing is formation diversification, the ability to change formation strength readily by varying the position of the backs and wide receivers. During the Sixties we set our defense against two tight ends and had split-end adjustments (Chapter 1). As split-end offenses become the rule rather than the exception, an important change in defens've philosophy will be required. The basic defense will have to be aligned against split-end sets, with necessary adjustments to the double tight-end alignment. We have done some interesting experimenting with this problem and find several exciting alternatives available.

Since our basic split-end adjustments were discussed in Chapter 1, we will first evaluate the problems of incorporating multiple coverages and defending the Wishbone in our basic defense before exploring possible future trends for the Invert Defense.

MULTIPLE COVERAGES

Utilization of multiple coverages is a simple matter for any four-deep alignment such as the Invert Defense. In fact, in Chapter 6, we indicated that we occasionally used the Hammer, 3/4 Rotate and Lock-On adjustments. If desired, these "adjustments" can be incorporated into the basic Invert scheme by introducing the popular titles of Strong and Free Safety for the inverts. The Strong Safety flip-flops to the formation strength and the Safeties "cock," pre-invert, if the formation is to the wide side of the field. The Strong Safety would have a preferred Slam call, invert action, on flow his way, while the Free Safety would prefer to Hammer, 3/4 Rotate, on action to his side, as diagrammed in Figure 10-1.

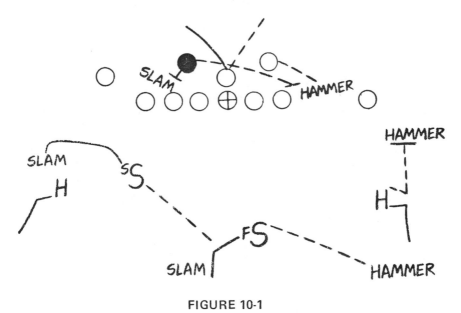

FIGURE 10-1

Slam/Hammer Reactions on Flow

Utilizing an "Eagle" or 43-type linebacker, flat responsibility can be exchanged for the backer's normal hook/curl responsibility on a Bang call. The Safety merely squats in the hook zone reading the tight receiver, ready to steal the look-in pass, slide to the curl or revert on bootleg action, as we'll explain in more detail later. Figure 10-2 shows the Bang call against a quick pass.

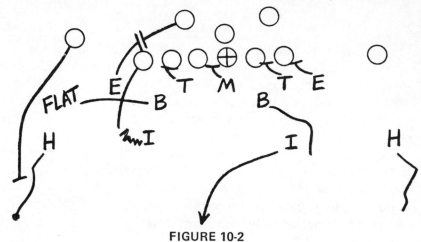

FIGURE 10-2

Bang Call vs. Quick Pass

The Slam, Hammer and Bang calls can easily be coordinated into a single scheme of coverage if a variety of coverages is desired. A call is made on each side by the invert to his respective HB and linebacker. On the snap, a frontside is established by movement of a key, normally the middle-back. The side that the key goes to implements its call, while the backside employs a standard backside coverage with invert to the deep-middle, HB to the deep-outside and linebacker cushioning the backside. Figures 10-3 and 10-4 show how the frontside might develop to or away from the strength of the formation.

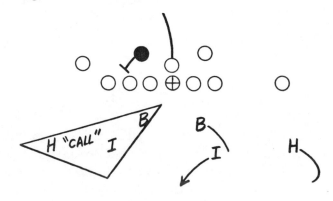

FIGURE 10-3

Frontside to Formation Strength

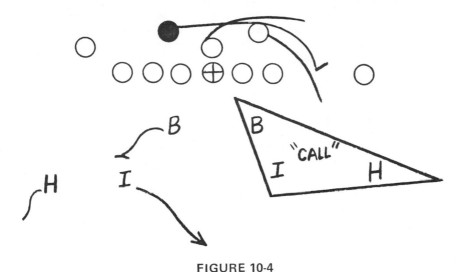

FIGURE 10-4

Frontside away from Formation Strength

While expanding the basic Invert Secondary to include Slam, Hammer and Bang calls requires no additional teaching, the inclusion of other coverages does. The extent to which a coach feels they are required should determine how many and which coverages should be added to his basic coverage. We feel strongly that *only* needed coverages should be added, even against outstanding passing teams. Practice and teaching time should be proportional to the time a coverage is used in a game. A slightly used coverage, therefore, would merit little practice time, and hence would prove more harmful than helpful.

We feel that there is a place for pure man coverage on some goal line and blitzing situations. A Lock-on, Safety-Free Zone, while weak against option attacks, provides excellent short and medium pass coverage, and can be an effective change-off from the Invert Zone. Against sets with two or more wide receivers, the combination of 5 Short Zones under 2-Deep, and Lock-on under a 2-Deep can be a valuable addition to the Invert defensive scheme. Each of these coverages is readily adaptable to the Invert personnel. They are included in this text not as a description of what was done by us with the Invert Defense in the Sixties, but as speculation of what will be done during the coming decade.

Man Coverage (Figure 10-5)

1. *Use:* With any multiple stunt or goal-line running situation.
2. *Stance and Alignment:* As close to basic Invert alignment as offensive formation will allow.
3. *Keys and Initial Movement:* Read through receiver for run/pass. Support run from normal angle, cover man on pass.
4. *Technique:* Since you can not envelop a receiver, you must take away two sides, deep and out, or inside and under, and play through the receiver to the other sides. In pure man coverage, the deep routes must be eliminated on alignment, so we play behind and in or behind and out. Never allow a receiver to get squared-up, or he will have the advantage of both inside and outside cuts.
5. *Responsibilities:* As diagrammed.
6. *Adjustments:* "Combo" two receivers aligned less than five yards apart. "Switch" on motion as receivers assume new order of receiving threats.

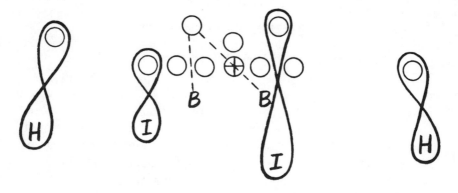

FIGURE 10-5

Lock-on, Safety Free Zone (Figure 10-6)

1. *Use:* Excellent against short and medium pass threats, or deep patterns by wide-outs. Particularly effective against teams whose backs are not particularly effective receivers.
2. *Stance and Alignment:* Basic, with slight "cocking" of inverts.
3. *Keys and Initial Movement:* HBs and Strong Safety (*up* invert) key their immediate receiving threat for run/pass, and react accordingly. Free Safety, *deep* invert, reacts to ball and QB's eyes. Keep play in front of you, play center field on pass.
4. *Technique:* Aggressive man-to-man cover under free-safety zone.
5. *Responsibilities:* As diagrammed.

6.   *Adjustments:* "Switch" and "Combo" calls as in man coverage.

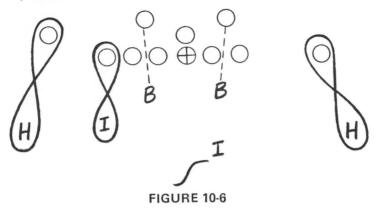

FIGURE 10-6

Lock-on, Double Safety Free Zone (Figure 10-7)

1.   *Use:* Against formations with two or more wide-outs, and in definite passing situations.
2.   *Stance and Alignment:* HBs walk up on wide receivers, assuming position one yard inside, or out, and three yards off ball. If outside alignment, outside foot should be up; if inside, the inside foot must be forward. Inverts align deeper and wider than normal in position to move to area of responsibility.
3.   *Key and Initial Movement:* Attempt to read through receiver to ball for initial run/pass reaction, but prime concern must be with release of receiver. Allow him to close the cushion, then "Bump and run." Inverts shuffle for deep-half while reading ball.
4.   *Technique:* Execution of the "bump and run" is in two phases. First allow receiver to close cushion, maintaining an inside or outside position on him. Deliver an aggressive blow through him as he passes, following through right into his stride. Now, "run" with him, mirroring his moves and playing the ball as described in the Turn and Run Drill (Chapter 6).
5.   *Responsibilities:* HBs and linebackers play aggressive man coverage, while the inverts have deep-half zone responsibility.
6.   *Adjustments:* "Switch" and "Combo" calls are employed when required as with other coverages employing man-to-man duties.

Five Short, Two-Deep Zone (Figure 10-8)

1.   *Use:* As complement to Lock-on, Double Safety-Free. Used when the option or running play is also a threat. Excellent against short pass or run on corner, and because alignment is same as Lock-on, it discourages deep passes.

2. *Stance and Alignment:* Same as described for Lock-on, Double Safety Free.

3. *Key and Initial Movement:* Same as previously described through the "bump."

4. *Technique:* HB must first determine position of next receiving threat to his inside, so that he will know how long he can be involved in the "bump" process before releasing into his zone. On dropback or flow to you, open to the outside after the bump to protect the sideline. On flow away, open inside to best cushion your deep-half.

5. *Responsibilities:* Zones as diagrammed.

6. *Adjustments:* (1) Don't go inside after a tight receiver, play as a corner LB. (b) On motion to you, loosen as motion man crosses your initial position.

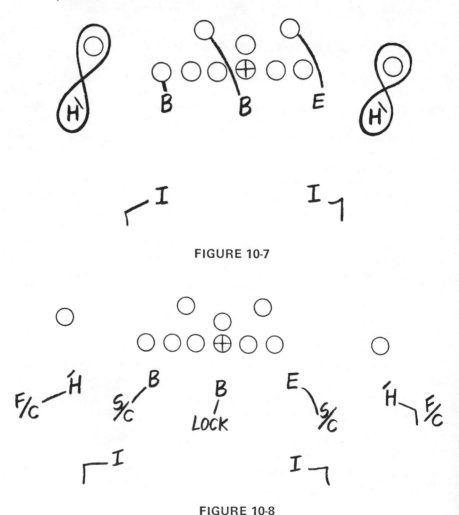

FIGURE 10-7

FIGURE 10-8

Our explanation of multiple coverages here is purposely brief, including only the basic information required to show how they can be incorporated into the Invert Defense. We have not been convinced by the high school offenses we have faced at the date of this writing that multiple coverages are necessary, but admit that it is becoming increasingly apparent that they soon will be. When they are definitely needed, it will be important for the coach to have them already incorporated into his defensive scheme. Defensive backs can be taught a variety of skills and techniques, but as the number of skills is increased, the degree of competence is likely to show a decrease. On the other hand, when the offense runs "veer" action off-tackle, and the tight end releases down the seam (Figure 10-9), the Invert Defense is put to real stress. If *your* opponent can successfully complete this pass with any degree of consistency, you had better have an alternate coverage to employ or you are going to get beaten.

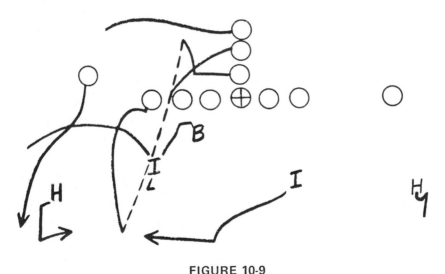

FIGURE 10-9

Quick Pass vs. Invert Defense

We could, within the context of our basic Invert Defense, defend this play *if* we "had the chalk last," but on the field we must be ready to defend it *now*. If we can do it with our personnel in the Invert Zone, we would; if not, we'll be ready with a variation in coverage. Be it a Bang call, Lock-on or any other, we will be ready.

DEFENDING THE WISHBONE OFFENSE

For the sake of discussion we will assume that the basic Wishbone offense is composed of (1) the Triple Option, (2) the Counter Option, (3) Counter Dive, (4) Off-Tackle Power Play and (5) Play-Action Passes. The most significant strength of this offense, we feel, is that all of those plays begin identically. The Triple Option itself requires the most specific defensive concentration. The other plays simply represent a chess game in which the opponent attempts to determine what you are doing to successfully defend the Triple, if you are, and employs the counter or alternate that will give you the most trouble.

Four "Musts" in Defending the Triple Option

1. Definite assignments for FB, QB and pitcn.
2. At least two men assigned to fullback.
3. Determine a preferred outside ballcarrier (QB or pitch).
4. Use stunts to make QB read more difficult.

With the Invert Defense, the man who probably never makes a tackle on the Triple Option is our most important defender. The Mikeman must be particularly aggressive against this series, so that he can force the offense to block him with the guard to the side of the play. If the guard is looping into the play and the guard releases for the linebacker, we feel that Mike should be able to get a good piece of the fullback, and if not tackling him, at least force the "crease" a little deeper. We rarely offset Mike against Triple Option teams, so they can not predict his loop direction. As Mike scoops, he looks for the fullback and guard's block. If FB comes his way, he fights to him; if FB goes opposite, he squares up to defend the Counter Dive. Figure 10-10 shows Mike's play against the Triple Option and Counter.

With the assist of Mike, the tackle and linebacker have basic responsibility for the FB. The fact that the tackle may be on an inside or outside loop makes blocking by the offensive tackle more difficult. While his assignment may be clear, the footwork involved in blocking a tackle on an inside loop is quite different from that involved in blocking a "shuffle" linebacker. Whether the call is Monster or Chuckles, the basic responsibility for the tackle and LB will always be "fullback" (Figure 10-11).

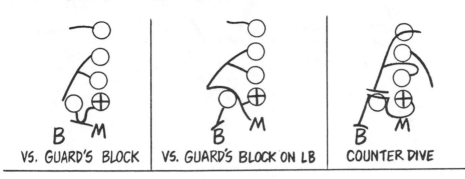

| VS. GUARD'S BLOCK | VS. GUARD'S BLOCK ON LB | COUNTER DIVE |

FIGURE 10-10

Mike's Play vs. the Triple Option

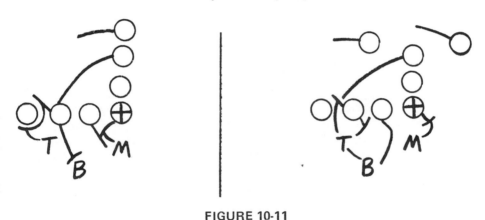

FIGURE 10-11

T/LB vs. Fullback, Chuckles, Monster

Basic end responsibility is always QB, regardless of the loop direction. The man with flat responsibility, normally the *up* invert, is responsible for the pitch. The entire picture, therefore, would look like Figure 10-12 a and b to the tight end's side.

On the SE's side, the responsibility would vary with the alignment of the split-end adjustment called. Of course in the "normal" alignment, which we would use most often against a Wishbone team because of the basically balanced nature of their attack, there would be no difference in responsibility from that diagrammed for the TE side. In an Eagle call, the end and LB would exchange duties (Figure 10-13), while on a Cover call, the end and invert (Figure 10-14) would exchange duties.

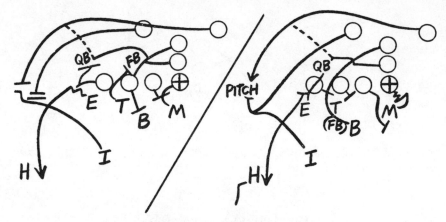

FIGURE 10-12 (a and b)

Triple Option to TE's side

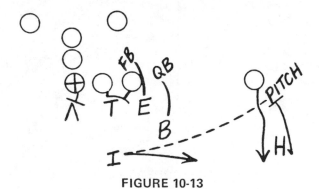

FIGURE 10-13

Triple Option vs. "Eagle"

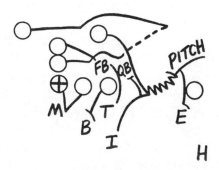

FIGURE 10-14

Triple Option vs. "Cover" Adjustment

Our concern for the relative running ability of the QB and pitchman will determine how aggressively we play the QB. The sooner the pitch is made, the more running room the tailback has. If the QB is our first concern, we will make a definite and aggressive hit on the QB. We want the good-running QB to have no option at all. If, on the other hand, the pitchman has exceptional speed, our defensive end will "cat and mouse" him, keeping his outside leg back and ready to pursue the pitch. The wider we can force the QB to run, the less running room remains available for the pitchman.

We do not feel that any single corner defense is adequate against the Triple Option. A most important phase of our defense, then, is stunting on the corner. We use three different stunts to change our option responsibility, besides our basic loop to the right or left. The Blood call, as described in Chapter 1, is used when we are primarily concerned with the handoff to the FB. The LB and DE change responsibilities as in Figure 10-15.

The opposite of a Blood call would be a Veer call, in which the end goes out to the pitch, the tackle takes the QB and the invert squats, as on "bang" to support the LB on the fullback, if necessary, and then supports the play from inside-out. We generally reserve the Veer call for longer yardage situations when we suspect that the QB is thinking "Get wide" (Figure 10-16).

Finally the loop tackle and end may exchange duties with an "X" stunt. The obvious result is shown in Figure 10-17.

As we indicated in the beginning of this section, the problem of defending the Wishbone is not always the Triple Option, but defending its companion plays after making a commitment to the Triple. To diagram each play here would serve no particular purpose, but we feel that we have provided for the basics of defending the companion plays by giving "counter" responsibility to our backside linebacker, and "revert" reactions to our inverts, allowing them time to revert against Counter-Option action. The deep-outside position of our HBs places them in the best position to defend against the play action pass, and we just hope that our football players can butt heads as well as our opponents when it comes time to defend the off-tackle power play. In effect, we feel that we have within the scheme of the Invert Defense the tools to defend the Wishbone offense. In fact, because it is a 3-back offense, without the benefit of crackback blockers to each side, the invert is *the* most desirable defensive alignment.

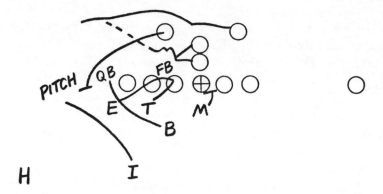

FIGURE 10-15

Monster Blood vs. Triple Option

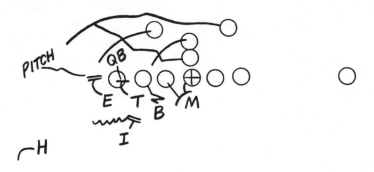

FIGURE 10-16

Chuckles Veer vs. Triple Option

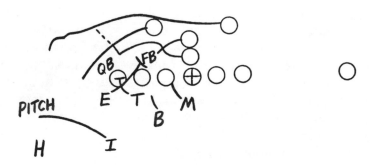

FIGURE 10-17

Chuckles "X" vs. Triple Option

OFFSETTING THE TREND TOWARD SPLIT-END OFFENSES

As offenses tend more and more toward using a split-end, we must reach the point where we consider the split-end set as a basic and two tight-ends as the exception. Quite frankly, we can not wait for this to be the case. We mentioned in Chapter 1 that we felt the split-end sets had certain inherent limitations, particularly in their ability to attack the off-tackle area to the split-end's side. Defensively we feel that we can remove a lineman from the defensive line as we did with the Hawk Defense (Chapter 7), and utilize that man with a greater degree of flexibility.

The biggest advantage of this move would be the variety of defensive fronts that could evolve, taking greater advantage of hashmark tendencies. We can see where the 43, 44 and 50 fronts could be integrated into a workable "stunting" front that could create havoc for most any high school's blocking rules. The diagrams in Figure 10-18 give an indication of what we project might be the multiple fronts available to us against split-end sets, and the necessary adjustments to tight end sets.

The preceding diagrams are working drawings. We have started with what we believe we'd like to see against split-end sets, and work backward to the adjustments necessary for two tight ends. We are not yet satisfied with some of the problems that appear in teaching multiple techniques to inverts, linebackers and ends, but we think that we have a start. By the time that split-end offenses are the rule rather than the exception, we expect that these problems will have been solved.

Before we look for answers to problems that don't already exist, it seems more important to review the problems that are already upon us.

THE MOST DIFFICULT PLAYS FOR THE INVERT DEFENSE

The "Offense of the Seventies," as we see it, will no doubt incorporate those plays, patterns and blocking schemes that have been most successful against the Invert Defense in the past. We must first recognize that personal pride prevents any Defensive Coach from suggesting that this is the way to beat us. We can and probably will be beaten by the better players far more often than we will by plays. But we think that the following plays are the ones that have given us the biggest problems and place maximum stress on the Invert Defense.

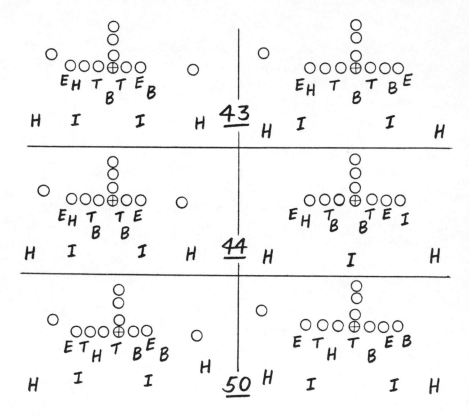

FIGURE 10-18

Multiple Fronts vs. SE Offenses/Adj. to 2 TE's

The Toughest Pass Plays:

Quick Pass to the Tight End

As diagrammed in Figure 10-9, we feel that this play is probably the most potent short pass against the pure Invert Defense *if* the offense's off-tackle play is respected. The off-tackle threat impairs the ability of the DT and DE from holding up the TE's release. Initial concern with the run holds the linebacker from assuming a good undercover position, and the flanker's wide spread produces a broad "seam" for the completion between the HB and *deep* invert.

Of course, pre-inverting to formation and field, a correct read by the linebacker and/or an adequate hold-up by the DE can result in a crucial interception. Similarly, a Bang call or Lock-on coverage will almost assure the Hawk of interception if the pass is thrown. Of course, respect for this play tends to weaken the off-tackle defense. That is what makes the game interesting.

Bootleg Pass

The basic Bootleg Pass pattern puts a strain on the undercoverage of all defenses. The responsibility for defending against the Drag pattern falls to the linebackers in the Invert Defense as in most others. We can cover this play on paper (Figure 10-19), but on the field it is often a different story.

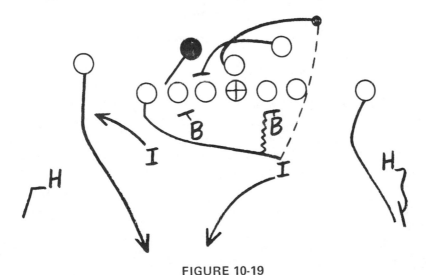

FIGURE 10-19

Bootleg Pass vs. the Invert Defense

The use of the Bang call has added a new dimension to our ability to defend the Bootleg. We could not expect an invert on an *up* reaction to revert on Bootleg and get back into the deep-middle; however, on the Bang call he initially squats in the hook zone, reads for Bootleg, and easily reverts back to the deep-middle. The invert originally *deep* can revert back along the Invert Triangle and be in excellent position to cover the TE running a Drag pattern (Figure 10-20). Again, we can cover the play with our basic invert action, but the Bang call offers an attractive alternative.

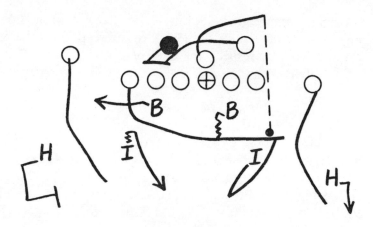

FIGURE 10-20

Bang Call vs. Bootleg Pass

Quick Bootleg, Wingback Square-out

Flat coverage opposite the action of the inverts is assuredly a weak area for the Invert Defense. We have found, however, that most teams attack this area with an inside receiver, TE or slotback, after clearing with the wide receiver. We can usually handle that play very well, but when that pattern is reversed, off a backfield action that most likely will draw the inverts to the opposite side, we have a real problem getting into the passing lane (Figure 10-21).

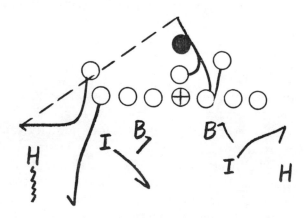

FIGURE 10-21

Quick Bootleg Pass, WB Square-out

We have successfully countered this play in the past by "switching" flat responsibility from the tackle to the end (Figures 3-6 and 3-7). Since the corner is not challenged, the tackle can adequately contain. Secondly, we have keyed, and will continue to key, the wingback in passing situations.

Double Hook/Backside Seam Pass

Probably the most effective dropback pass pattern against our Invert Scheme has been the double hook pattern on the frontside and a weak "post" on the backside (Figure 10-22). The double hook neutralizes our "hook to curl" teaching of our linebackers, as he must stay inside to defend the tight receiver on the "hook." The invert covering the flat tends to get width and depth to cushion the sideline, leaving the "curl" area vulnerable. At the same time, the most difficult receiver for an invert to defend is the end running a post pattern on the "heels of his retreat" to the deep-middle zone. The invert must sprint to the middle of his zone, square up and then skate facing back to his principal threat.

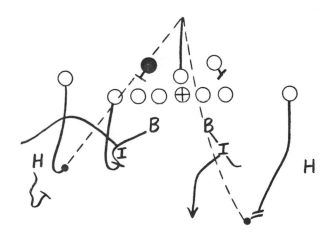

FIGURE 10-22

Invert Defense vs. the Double Hook/Post Pass

There are no real adjustments to suggest against this pass, as the Invert Zone is, on paper, sound against it. The fact is, however, that it truly tests the cushion of the *up* invert and the retreat of the *deep* invert. It demonstrates the necessity for *communication* in the secondary. The *deep* invert and backside HB can easily defend the post if they play it, and the *up* invert can cushion the "curl" as easily as the sideline if he is playing it. This play highlights all of the concepts that were presented in the Pyramid of Pass Defense (Figure 6-1), and is a good indicator of how effectively the Invert Secondary is being played.

The Toughest Running Plays:

The Invert Defense is not without difficulties against the running game also, but as it was with the passing game, it is most often the quality of the individual players, not the plays, that provides the greatest challenge. The following plays have traditionally given us the biggest problems:

Isolation Play to Side of Loop

When a good double-team block cuts off the scoop of the Mikeman, the natural path of the loop tackle creates an excessively large hole for the LB to defend (Figure 10-23). Teams with good blocking backs can effectively attack this way when they guess right on the line slant and are not fooled by a stunt in the area.

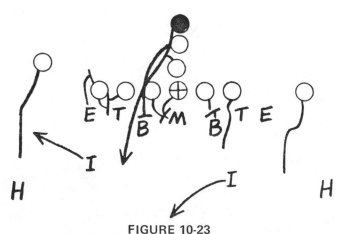

FIGURE 10-23

Isolation Play vs. Invert Defense

Counter Dive (Fold Block) Against the Loop

The "counter" reaction by our linebackers is the most difficult one. In discussing linebacker play (Chapter 4), we indicated that we had attempted several ways to teach the counter reaction. We feel that our present technique of stepping up on the guard is best, but it is easier said than done. The linebackers' natural aggressive tendencies must be well disciplined or the Counter Dive (Figure 10-24) will be real trouble.

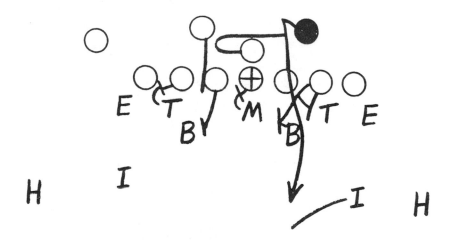

FIGURE 10-24

Counter Dive (Fold Block)

The Counter Trap from Power "I"

The Counter Trap play combines some of the advantages of isolation blocking with effective counter-action. Figure 10-25 shows one example that we feel is most difficult. Because it breaks against the grain, it can easily become a gig gainer. Stunts and variation in slant direction are the invert's best method for stopping plays of this type.

Speed Option on the Corner

We suggested earlier in the text that the best way to attack the corner was to set a flanker four to seven yards outside, or a slot formation with the end split that distance from the slot. This gives him an excellent crackback angle on the invert and the two can combine for a crackback/peel combination block on the corner. We think that the Speed-Option (Figure 10-26) is one of the best ways to get on the corner behind that blocking scheme.

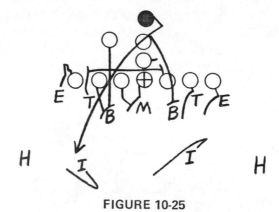

FIGURE 10-25

Power "I" Counter Trap

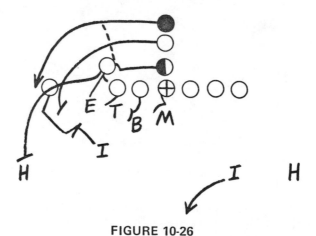

FIGURE 10-26

Speed-Option (Crackback/Peel Block)

In effect, we have attempted to show in this section how we think the Invert Defense may be vulnerable, and in particular, how we anticipate that it will be attacked during the coming decade. We are sure that each and every coach who reads it, would quickly add or delete some of the ideas in accordance with his particular philosophy. Our point, however, is that the Invert Defense is not static, and that it will continue to evolve as change is dictated by trends in offensive football. Within its structure are the sound foundations upon which change can be successfully produced.

11

Coaching by the Numbers
for Invert Defensive Success

"Statistics are for losers. The only numbers that count are those in the final score." How often have you heard those words from a member of the coaching fraternity commenting on the apparent wasted effort of a coaching colleague who has dutifully tabulated data on his team's performance?

FOUR INGREDIENTS IN THE WINNING FORMULA

Like most coaches seeking the "formula of success," we have searched diligently for the key to producing winning football teams. It is readily apparent that no single offense, defense or strategy of play is "best" for all of us. Furthermore, coaches of very divergent philosophies and personalities have made repeated trips to the winner's circle. We have concluded that there may be no single way to win: that each of the coaches who has won regularly has found, for him, a balance of the four necessary ingredients, and most importantly, discovered a bonding agent that works best for his particular situation. Numbers, goals, statistics, tendencies, breakdowns and outlines of some form, have proven to be our bonding agent at River Dell during our reign with the Invert Defense. We seem always to be relating things with some statistical study or numbered outline. We don't mean to imply that numbers will work for you, but they have for us—probably because we believed in them, and have made them work.

1. *Program:* Without a doubt, the basic ingredient all winning formulas possess is "program," a term difficult to describe in specifics but easily recognizable in the finished product. To us, a good program means achieving maximum utilization of the personnel, facilities and resources available through your school, community and "friends."

It is not our purpose in this text to describe our overall total program, but it is necessary to recognize that successful defense can not be separated from the whole scheme of things. We have attempted to include those aspects of our program that directly relate to playing sound defense—particularly in Chapter 2 where we discussed staff responsibilities and incorporating the defense into the practice plan, and in Chapter 5, in which we showed how all available data is incorporated into a meaningful game plan.

We have not included our scouting system, however, because it is similar to that of most teams, and works for us only because it is tailor-made for the personnel on our staff. Similarly, we have refrained from discussing specific non-football duties of our coaches, although they play an important role in our program, because they apply to our particular situation. To suggest that it is desirable to have an assistant in track or wrestling may be a good idea in one system, and a very poor one in another. Maximum utilization is necessary, but understandably unique for each school.

2. *Understanding:* An obvious prerequisite to teaching something well is thorough understanding of the subject by the teacher. It was our goal when we began this manuscript to provide our fellow coaches with a basis for complete understanding of our Invert Defense's philosophy, techniques and scheme of play. We felt that we had some ideas that we would like to share with others. While we may never know if we have achieved that goal, we have benefited from personal satisfaction of much greater significance. First was the realization that what we had been doing was, in fact, as sound as we had always felt it was. It had stood the test of thorough examination. Secondly, many things we just "did," without really understanding why, had to be evaluated

before we could put them in print. The result was a far greater understanding of what we were doing, and a much deeper appreciation of the defensive system that had worked for us in producing a record of 54-17-1.

Technical competence is but one-half of understanding. Of at least equal importance, or more, is understanding of the athletes. A great bit of advice that I heard at one football clinic was to "put names with the X's and O's. Be sure that the young man playing the position is capable of doing what is asked of him." Understanding is the basis of the coach-player relationship, and that relationship is as important to success as any other aspect we might consider. Again, there is no single way for that relationship to be, except that it be natural and based on common respect for one another.

3. *Communication:* This is the area in which every coach can improve steadily during his coaching career. It is a personal area, because we would all like to believe that we are doing an excellent job of communicating our ideas to the players. If they don't respond properly to them, we tend to think that we are coaching very stupid or incapable players, when often the fact is that we have not adequately communicated their responsibilities to them, or we have not provided them with practice experiences to prepare them for their tasks. Our Player's Manual includes in the introduction some advice to the players on how to distinguish a winner from a loser:

HOW TO TELL A WINNER FROM A LOSER

1. A winner says, "Let's find out"; a loser says, "Nobody knows."
2. When a winner makes a mistake, he says, "I was wrong, I'll get it next time"; when a loser makes a mistake, he makes an excuse.
3. A winner goes through a problem; a loser goes around it, but never gets past it.
4. A winner makes commitments; a loser makes promises.
5. A winner says, "I'm good, but not as good as I ought to be"; a loser says, "I'm not as bad as a lot of others."
6. A winner tries to learn from those who are better than he; a loser tears down those who are better.

These statements are as applicable to the coaches as they are to the players, particularly in the area of communication. Every season we have found better ways to communicate our ideas to the players. That is one reason why we rewrite the entire Defensive Manual each year. If that job has to be done, you are more willing to make changes for the better. Hopefully, this book will provide you, in some way, with better ideas for teaching your players. That is its primary purpose.

4. *Motivation:* The fourth and final ingredient in our winning formula is motivation. Again, we tread on an area that depends on human factors, and can not suggest that there is a right or wrong way. We feel that a coach must earn the respect of his athletes, and that his team will reflect his own personality. We suggested in the beginning of the chapter that we have had success with numbers, and, in fact, we have. Victory is something that must be earned and worked for. To achieve that ultimate victory, we must establish measurable guidelines along the way to rekindle the fires that motivate each of us.

We have meticulously recorded and preserved our statistics, good and bad alike, over the years. They have come out at many times in many ways to help us toward our goal. Our Defensive Standards of Excellence, team records, are kept up to date and in some seasons are a part of the Defensive Manual, and in other seasons have been posted in the locker room. If appropriate facilities were available, they would surely be posted in a place of honor for all to see, to serve as a constant reminder of the high standards we are working to achieve (Figure 11-1).

At the conclusion of each season, individual and team defensive statistics are compiled and distributed at the Annual Football Banquet. We want each player and our fans to have clear-cut evidence of the achievements of the squad (Figure 11-2). In addition, outstanding players will have their names added to future editions of the Defensive Manual as "former stars" at their position. As do so many teams, we use stars, hawks, etc., to reward outstanding play, but the most important source of team pride and motivation is our Defensive Bulletin Board.

DEFENSIVE BULLETIN BOARD

As it is with most team bulletin boards, ours serves the duel role of motivation and evaluation (Figure 11-3). It generally presents a valid description of what is happening on the field, indicating the areas in which you are and are not doing the job. Admittedly, there can be times when its data is deceptive, but over the long run, it truly tells the story.

The Defensive Honor Roll centers the Bulletin Board. It lists each player who will play on the varsity defense, and stars are placed in the appropriate blocks for Defensive Player of Week, Hawks (interceptions), Claws (fumble recoveries), Caused H/C (caused hawk or claw with rush or tackle), and Key Tackles. It takes a great deal of effort by the respective assistant coaches and student statisticians to keep check on all of this data, but the motivational rewards to the players make it all worthwhile.

Our Rushing Defense Chart (Figure 11-4) graphically shows where the offense attacked us on every play of the game, and how much was gained on each play. We compile the weekly information at the bottom of the chart to provide running totals for the season. When a passer is tackled for a loss, or on a broken play where a definite hole has not been established, the loss will be recorded in the area closest to the original position of the tackler.

RIVER DELL HIGH SCHOOL FOOTBALL
DEFENSIVE STANDARDS OF EXCELLENCE

UNDEFEATED — '64, '67, '70
SHUTOUT VICTORIES — 4 each in '66, '67, '70, '71
DEFENSE vs. SCORING — 32 points (3.5/game) in '70
TOTAL DEFENSE   927 yards (103/game) in '71
RUSHING DEFENSE — 521 yards (57.8/game) in '71
PASSING DEFENSE — 360 yards (40/game) in '68
PASS COMPLETION % — 32% (50/156) in '70, 32% (35/108) in '66
HAWK (interception) % — 18.1% (19/105) in '71
                        17.2% (27/156) in '70

Note: We have intercepted at least 1 pass for every 2 completed during the '66, '67, '68, '70 and '71 seasons.

HAWKS RETURNED FOR TDs — 3 in '70
RD SCORES ON PUNT RETURNS — 6 in '66
OPPONENTS avg. PUNT RETURN — 1.2 yds in '66
PRIDE % — 92% in '67
3rd DOWN % — 76.2% in '70

FIGURE 11-1
River Dell High School Football
Defensive Standards of Excellence

* 9 Wins   0 Losses
* 4 Shutouts (Lodi 6-0, Pas. Hills 36-0, In. Hills 32-0, N. High 22-0)
Statistically we were the No. 1 Defensive team in Bergen County.
* Gave up 32 pts. for avg. of 3.5 per game.
  Gave up 5 TDs (one each in the 5 non-shutouts)
* Opponents Rushing Yardage   591 yds   65.7 per game.
  Opponents Passing Yardage   675 yds   75.0 per game.
* Opponents Total Offense   1266 yds   140.7 per game.

PRIDE % (preventing TD after opponent crossed 20-yd. line) 80%
* 3rd Down % (preventing 1st Down on 3rd situation) 76.2%
          —opponents avg. gain of 1.6 yds. on 3rd down—

DEFENSIVE GOALS

We have seven defensive goals for each game. They are Victory (9/9), Shutout (4/9), Under 100 yds. Rushing (8/9), Under 90 yds. Passing (6/9), Combination of 3 Hawks or Claws (8/9), 67% 3rd Success (9/9), 100% Pride Defense (6/9). We accomplished 7 of 7 goals in 3 games, and 50 of the 63 goals for the season.

It is ironic that we did not set a school record in the yards passing category, as Pass Defense was our strong suit this season.

* Our opponents completed 32% of their passes (50/156).
* We intercepted 17.2% of our opponents passes (we intercepted more than 1 for every 2 passes completed).
* We had 27 Hawks (interceptions) and 10 Claws (fumble recovery).
* We scored 3 TDs on interceptions, and set up *many* others.

INDIVIDUAL

Chris Van Wagoner limited opponents to a net gain of -11 yds in 42 running plays around his end. He intercepted a pass for a 70-yrd. TD, caused 4 Hawks with his pass rush and had 15 tackles for losses.

Juniors Sal Comarato and Kevin Looram combined efforts on their side of the line to limit opponents to -17 yds in 22 running plays. Sal caused 2 Hawks while Kevin got 3 Hawks.

Senior halfbacks Dave Lake and George Horton each tied the school record of 6 individual interceptions—George getting 3 of his in one game, tying another record, while Dave returned two of his Hawks for TDs—a new record.

We will all certainly remember the fine season of football at River Dell this year and particularly we'll remember the efforts of the Seniors who made our defense #1: Chris Van Wagoner, Paul DeMaio, Jim Scanlon, Mike Tfank, Doug Gray, Glenn Baker, Dave Lake, George Horton, and Kevin Collier.

* Indicates school record.

FIGURE 11-2

1970 River Dell Defensive Statistics

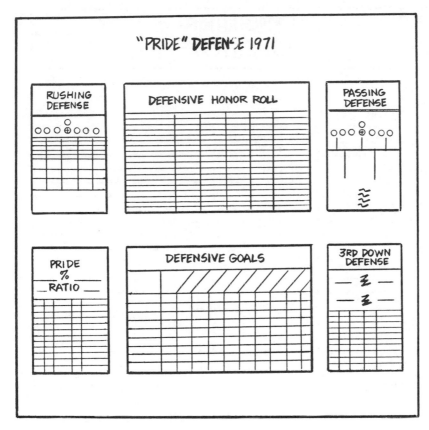

FIGURE 11-3
Defensive Bulletin Board

The Rushing Chart has been responsible for a great deal of positive rivalry among our defensive players. You can rest assured that the right tackles are not only aware of the rushing statistics in their own immediate area, but are equally conversant with the data from the opposite side of the line.

The Passing Defense Chart (Figure 11-5) has been selected for use on the Bulletin Board because of its similarity to the Rushing Chart and its graphic presentation of the passing game. As coaches, we are more concerned with reading the information available in Figure 11-8, but the players respond more favorably to this one. It shows the area in which all passes were thrown, completions, interceptions and the overall passing statistics for the game and for the season.

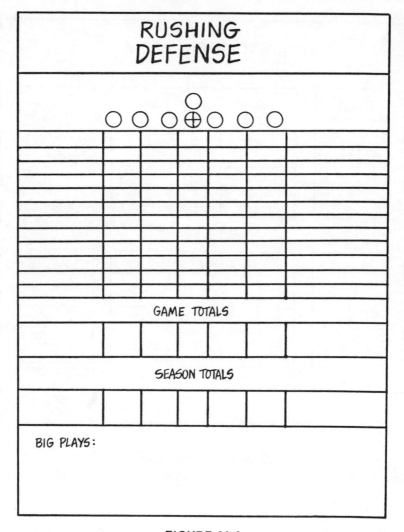

FIGURE 11-4

Rushing Defense Chart

Several seasons ago we initiated a motivational concept which has proven extremely valuable to us. We simply divided the field into three zones, using the 20-yard lines, the Pride Lines, as the dividing lines. We suggested that most of the game was played between the 20's, but that winning and losing were decided by the way teams performed between the 20-yard line and the goal line. We expect everybody on our team, and our fans as well, to

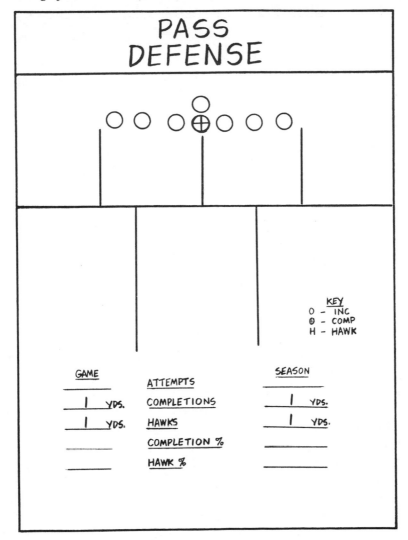

FIGURE 11-5

Passing Defense Chart

recognize these Pride Lines. When the ball reaches the Pride Line, our boys reach down for that little extra, whether we are on offense or defense. The Pride % Chart (Figure 11-6) shows the game and season percentage/attempt ratio, and is followed by a breakdown of what happened on each play in the Pride Zone in that particular game.

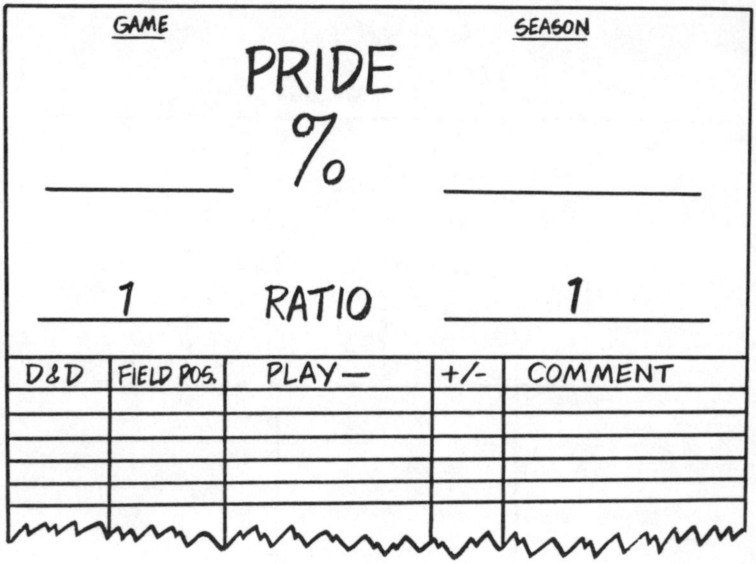

FIGURE 11-6

Pride % Chart

The defense's principal function is to turn the ball over to the offensive unit. Pro football has made each and every fan fully aware of the significance of the 3rd down. As we attempted to capitalize with an emotional edge in the Pride Zone, we want to develop a similar "lift" for the 3rd down play. Our 3rd Down Chart (Figure 11-7) is designed to indicate our percentage of success in this area, as well as to show specifically the results of this play in each game.

We should point out that we will evaluate the 4th down play rather than the 3rd when the ball is in four-down territory. The percentage is actually the ratio of times that we have accomplished our goal of forcing the ball to be turned over, whether it be by punt on the succeeding down or with a Hawk.

The final and most revealing chart on our Defensive Board is the Defensive Goal Chart. It is similar to most other charts on goals in that the goals are listed down the side of the chart, the games across the top. The appropriate blocks are colored in in gold if the goal is achieved and in black if it is not. While this probably reveals more about the game itself than anything else, it is not, we feel, a good motivator because it is too broad based. The other

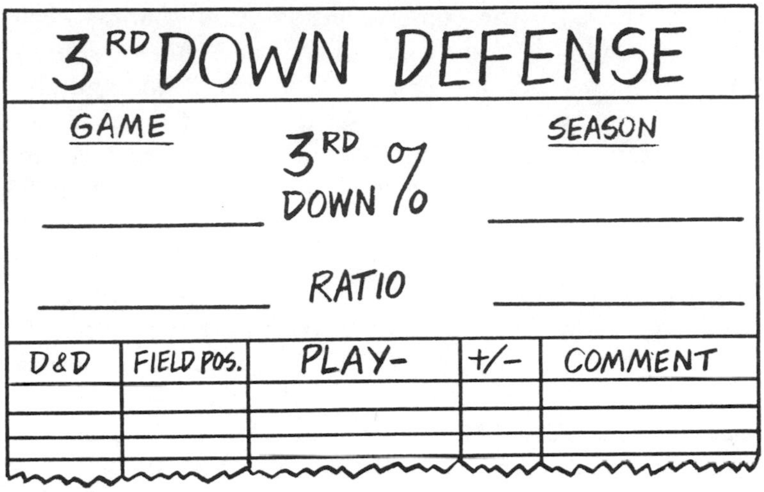

```
┌─────────────────────────────────────────────────┐
│  3ᴿᴰDOWN DEFENSE                                  │
│  GAME          3ᴿᴰ  o7        SEASON              │
│                DOWN /o                            │
│  _____               _____            │
│                RATIO                              │
│  _____               _____            │
├──────┬─────────┬──────────┬──────┬───────────────┤
│ D&D  │FIELD POS.│ PLAY-    │ +/-  │ COMMENT        │
├──────┼─────────┼──────────┼──────┼───────────────┤
│      │         │          │      │               │
│      │         │          │      │               │
│      │         │          │      │               │
└──────┴─────────┴──────────┴──────┴───────────────┘
```

FIGURE 11-7

3rd Down Chart

charts zero in on a particular aspect; they help to bring a particular player's attention to a single area, or the entire team's attention to a single play. Goals are things to be analyzed before the contest is played and reviewed during the course of a season, as they provide general direction for our energies. With the exception of the shutout goal, they rarely come to mind during the game.

The Defensive Goals that we have used at River Dell are:

1. Victory
2. Shutout
3. Hold opponent under 100 yards rushing.
4. Hold opponent under 90 yards passing.
5. Get a combination of three or more Hawks and Claws.
6. 67% Success on 3rd Down.
7. 100% Success in the Pride Zone

EVOLUTION OF INVERT DEFENSE IS ROOTED IN NUMBERS

We have continually emphasized that the Invert Defense has been undergoing evolutionary changes since its inception. While most changes are rooted in the techniques of communication, most have been predicated on some statistical analysis. In Chapter 10, for example, we have left open the possibility of utilizing multiple coverages in the coming decade. This is not a decision that will be made by chance; it will be the result of studying a passing game chart that has been building steadily for a number of seasons. It is such a simple chart that it surprises me that we had not started tabulating it much earlier in our program. We simply record every forward pass thrown (Figure 11-8), including D&D, field position, pass action, receiver (or pattern), result and comments. We should therefore be able to recognize what particular pass plays, patterns, etc., have given us trouble over the years. If we evolve to multiple coverages, a column will be provided for the coverage called so that each coverage can be evaluated.

_____ OPP	DEFENSIVE PASSING GAME				DATE _____
D&D	FIELD POS.	ACTION	REC/PATTERN	RESULT	COMMENTS

FIGURE 11-8

Defensive Passing Game

Studies such as the one of pass defense can result in improvements in the techniques played, in stunts and variations used, and in overall strategy. As indicated in Chapter 3 in the section on the Outside Loop, we discovered that the area we thought would be strongest in our rushing defense had in fact become our weakest area because we were teaching a technique improperly. A revealing view of your defensive effectiveness, and of your philosophy, can be achieved each season by preparing a

Defensive Drive Chart at the conclusion of each season (Figure 11-9). This chart can prove very enlightening as a review of your defensive philosophy.

1971 DEFENSIVE DRIVE CHART						
FIELD POSITION (STARTING)	DRIVES	SCORES	PUNTS	TURNOVERS	DEF HELD	GAME END
G TO -20	23	1	14	5	1	2
-20 TO -40	43	3	22	17	1	–
-40 TO +40	17	2	7	5	1	2
+40 TO -20	3	–	–	1	2	–
-20 TO G	3	3	–	–	–	–

FIGURE 11-9

Defensive Drive Chart

Compilation of a Drive Chart, or other similar analysis, can provide a coach with material that can be used in motivation as well as technical football. The point is that "the basis of improvement" is available for the coach who looks hard enough for it.

INVERT DEFENSE AT COLLEGE LEVEL

Before completing this manuscript, we had the good fortune to be selected to join Coach Jim Root's football staff at the College of William and Mary. It was an opportunity that we had prepared for, and a challenge we desired. Our main concern was whether the things we had been teaching for eight years at the high school level were adaptable to the college game. I can say without reservation that *they can and do work*. At least 90 percent of the techniques and basic philosophies outlined in this text have been incorporated into our defensive plan. In the secondary, where we are specifically coaching, 98 percent of the skills, drills and process of communication are utilized. We have found a need to do some things at this level that we would not have considered had we continued to coach in high school. On the other hand, some of the small differences appear to be logical extensions of what we were doing, and have been included in the chapter dealing with the "Offense of the Seventies."

The Invert Defense is well suited for modern day football at any level. The one aspect of it that was as much responsible for our success at River Dell as any other factor is, in the beginning, missing here in college: *defensive pride.*

PRIDE

So much has been said by so many about this little word with the big meaning that it would probably be best to avoid it. But the fact is that we can not discuss the Invert Defense without recognizing that the pride shared by our players and coaches was responsible for our success.

Reading through the material that makes up this text, long after most of it has been prepared, is somewhat embarrassing. It sounds sometimes as if we "had all the answers," and the fact is that we do not. The Invert Defense is something that we grew with in the coaching profession. It has provided us with success, and for that we are thankful. We suspect that it can provide you with much of the same—*if* you can develop the PRIDE in it that we have.

Index